William Gallogly Moorehead

Studies in the Mosaic Institutions

the tabernacle, the priesthood, the sacrifices, the feasts of ancient Israel

William Gallogly Moorehead

Studies in the Mosaic Institutions
the tabernacle, the priesthood, the sacrifices, the feasts of ancient Israel

ISBN/EAN: 9783337090807

Printed in Europe, USA, Canada, Australia, Japan

Cover: Foto ©Lupo / pixelio.de

More available books at **www.hansebooks.com**

STUDIES

IN THE

MOSAIC INSTITUTIONS

THE TABERNACLE, THE PRIESTHOOD
THE SACRIFICES, THE FEASTS
OF ANCIENT ISRAEL

BY

W. G. MOOREHEAD, D.D.

PROFESSOR IN THE UNITED PRESBYTERIAN
THEOLOGICAL SEMINARY
XENIA, OHIO

"Others have labored, and ye are entered into their labor"
—*John 4:38, R.V.*

DAYTON, OHIO
W. J. SHUEY, PUBLISHER
1896

PREFACE

MUCH has been written on the Mosaic institutions—particularly on the tabernacle and the priesthood. Why add another book to the long list of those which treat of the same general subject? Two answers may be returned to this query. Twenty years ago a wide-spread interest prevailed as to the main features of ancient Judaism. Christians took great delight in its study. Models of the tabernacle were constructed and exhibited, and lectures were delivered to attentive audiences. For some years past this interest seems almost entirely to have subsided. Little concern for such studies is anywhere manifested. One aim of this little book is to help remove the apathy referred to, and to stimulate, with God's blessing, the minds of those who read it to a renewed interest and search into the books of Moses, that the prime truths touching God's way of saving sinners—unchangeably the same in all dispensations—may be apprehended in something of their fullness and preciousness.

Moreover, it cannot be denied that, by the attacks against the Mosaic authorship of the Pentateuch now so frequent and persistent, and by the efforts of the so-called "higher critics" to prove that Judaism, in its main features, is of comparatively recent date—that scarcely anything of the elaborate system existed at the time of Moses, not a few Christians have become perplexed and troubled, and hardly know what to think or believe. Now, if it can be shown that there was a *prophetic element in ancient Judaism;* that it was planned and established with the distinct aim to portray before the eyes of the chosen people God's gracious purposes with respect to the person and work of his Son, Jesus Christ our Lord,—if it can be shown that Judaism and Christianity bear to each other the relation of prediction and fulfillment, then Judaism was of God, was arranged and organized by an infinite Mind, that knows the future no less certainly than the present or the past, and, therefore, we may possess our souls in peace, and remain steadfast and unmovable in the presence of the skeptical assaults on the books of Moses; for if they are of God, they are inspired, genuine, and authoritative. If in any measure this little volume contributes to such an end, none will rejoice more than the author.

The author has availed himself of all the helps accessible to him in the preparation of these studies, among which may be more particularly specified Edersheim's "Temple Service," Cave's "Doctrine of Sacrifice," Oehler's "Biblical Theology" (by Professor Weidner), Fairbairn's "Typology," Jukes's "Law of the Offerings," Seiss's "Holy Types," and various commentaries. One book, which furnished both help and delight, deserves special mention: Dr. Andrew Bonar's Commentary on Leviticus, than which none is more reverential, spiritual, and able.

W. G. MOOREHEAD.

XENIA, OHIO, November 1, 1895.

CONTENTS

	PAGE
PREFACE,	iii
LIST OF ILLUSTRATIONS,	xi

CHAPTER I
INTRODUCTION

THE GOSPEL IN THE OLD TESTAMENT, - - - - - - 13

CHAPTER II
THE TABERNACLE OF THE WILDERNESS

I.	THE CONDITIONS OF WORSHIP,	31
II.	THE NAMES OF THE TABERNACLE,	34
III.	DESCRIPTION OF THE TABERNACLE,	36
IV.	THE POSITION OF THE TABERNACLE,	38
V.	THE COURT AND ITS CONTENTS,	40
	1. The Brazen Altar,	41
	(1) Its Form,	42
	(2) The Horns of the Altar,	44
	(3) The Position of the Altar,	46
	2. The Laver,	48
	(1) Its Material,	48
	(2) Its Form,	49
	(3) Its Position,	49
	(4) Its Typical Significance,	49
VI.	THE SANCTUARY AND ITS FURNITURE,	55
	1. The Candlestick,	56
	(1) Description,	56
	(2) Its Typical Meaning,	57
	2. The Table of Showbread,	62
	3. The Golden Altar of Incense,	66
	(1) The Place of This Altar in the Description of the Tabernacle and Its Furniture,	66
	(2) The Position of the Golden Altar,	69
	(3) The Incense Burned Upon the Altar,	70
	(4) The Connection of the Altar of Incense with the Altar of Sacrifice,	70
	(5) The Altar Symbolized Communion with God in Prayer and Worship,	71
	(6) The Altar Symbolized Prayer in Conjunction with Christ's Intercession,	72
	(7) The Altar Symbolized the Efficacy of Christ's Intercession,	73

CONTENTS

VI. THE SANCTUARY AND ITS FURNITURE, *continued.* PAGE
    4. The Veil, - - - - - - - - - 73
    5. The Ark of the Covenant, - - - - - - 75
        (1) The Cherubim, - - - - - - - 76
        (2) The Contents of the Ark, - - - - 78
        (3) The Ark God's Throne, - - - - - 79
        (4) The Mercy-Seat, - - - - - - 80
VII. TYPICAL SIGNIFICANCE OF THE TABERNACLE, - - - 82
    1. It Symbolized God's Presence with His Chosen People, - - - - - - - 83
    2. It Was Designed to Show the Identification of God with His Chosen Flock, - - - 83
    3. A Remarkable Illustration of God's Method of Bringing Sinners to Himself, - - - 85
    4. A Prophecy of Christ's Incarnation, - - - 88

CHAPTER III
THE PRIESTHOOD

I. THE UNIVERSALITY OF THE PRIESTLY OFFICE, - - 91
II. PRIESTHOOD A REAL OFFICE, - - - - - - 91
III. THE TWO GREAT PRIESTS OF THE OLD TESTAMENT, - 92
IV. THE HIGH PRIEST IN ISRAEL, - - - - - - 93
    1. The High Priest's Dress, - - - - - 95
        (1) The Ephod, - - - - - - - 95
        (2) The Breastplate, - - - - - - 96
        (3) The Miter and Golden Plate, - - - 98
        (4) Urim and Thummim, - - - - - 99
    2. The High Priest a Type of Christ, - - - 99
    3. The Functions of the High Priest, - - - 101
V. THE NATURE OF THE PRIESTLY OFFICE, - - - 105
    1. It Implies Choice, - - - - - - 105
    2. It Implies the Principle of Representation, - 106
    3. It Implies the Offering of Sacrifice, - - 109
    4. It Implies Intercession, - - - - - 111
    5. It Implies Action Toward God, - - - 113
VI. THE CONSECRATION OF AARON AND HIS SONS, - - 114
    1. Aaron and His Sons Shared in the Consecration, 114
    2. Their Washing with Water, - - - - 115
    3. The Investiture, - - - - - - - 115
    4. The Anointing of the High Priest, - - - 115
    5. The Bloodshedding and the Application of the Blood to the Priests, - - - - 120
    6. The Anointing of Aaron's Sons, - - - 121
    7. Retirement of the Priestly Family, - - - 122
    8. Priestly Blessing of the Chosen People, - - 123

CONTENTS vii

CHAPTER IV

THE SACRIFICES OFFERED AT THE BRAZEN ALTAR

GENERAL OBSERVATIONS, - - - - - - - - - 128
  1. The Prevalence of Sin, - - - - - - - 128
  2. God's Holiness, - - - - - - - - - 128
  3. God's Remedy for Man's Sin — Bloodshedding, - 129
  4. The Parties to the Sacrifice, - - - - - 131
  5. The Offerings of Leviticus Pictures of the One Supreme Offering of the Lord Jesus Christ, 131
  6. Classification of Offerings, - - - - - 132
  7. Order of Arrangement in Leviticus, - - - 133
  8. Ceremonial Perfection Required, - - - - 136

I. THE "SWEET-SAVOUR" OFFERINGS, - - - - - 138
  1. The Burnt-Offering, - - - - - - - 138
    (1) Its Varieties, - - - - - - - 139
    (2) Ceremony of the Offering, - - - - 139
    (3) The Nature of the Burnt-Offering, - - 141
    (4) The Typical Significance of the Burnt-Offering, - - - - - - - - - 143
  2. The Meat-Offering, - - - - - - - 147
    (1) Its Varieties, - - - - - - - 147
    (2) Its Materials, - - - - - - - 147
    (3) The Ceremonial of the Meat-Offering, - 149
    (4) The Nature of the Meat-Offering, - - 149
    (5) The Meat-Offering as a Type, - - - 151
  3. The Peace-Offering, - - - - - - - 158
    (1) Its Name, - - - - - - - - 158
    (2) Its Materials, - - - - - - - 159
    (3) Its Place, - - - - - - - - 161
    (4) Its Nature, - - - - - - - - 161
    (5) Its Spiritual Import, - - - - - 164
    (6) Qualifications of Partakers, - - - 166
    (7) The Offering Looked Forward and Backward, 167

II. THE SIN-SACRIFICES, - - - - - - - - 168
  1. Distinction Between Sin- and Trespass-Offerings, - 170
  2. The Sin-Sacrifice, - - - - - - - 171
    (1) Its Significance, - - - - - - 171
    (2) Its Varieties, - - - - - - - 172
  3. The Trespass-Offering, - - - - - - 177
  4. Fundamental Principles Embodied in These Sacrifices, - - - - - - - - 180
    (1) Substitution, - - - - - - - 180
    (2) Imputation, - - - - - - - 180
    (3) Vicarious Atonement, - - - - - 180
    (4) Propitiation, - - - - - - - 181

CHAPTER V

THE DAY OF ATONEMENT

I. THE DAY ITSELF, - - - - - - - - - - 183
   1. A Day of National Humiliation, - - - - 183
   2. It Imposed Most Solemn Anxieties and Severest Duties on the High Priest, - - - 184
   3. Special Services Performed by the High Priest Alone, - - - - - - - - 184
   4. Typical of Christ, - - - - - - - - 185
II. THE OFFERINGS OF THE DAY, - - - - - - - 185
   1. The Sin-Offering for the High Priest and His House, - - - - - - - - 186
   2. The Sin-Offering for the Congregation, - - - 187
   3. Transfer of the Sins of the Congregation to the Scapegoat, - - - - - - - 188
   4. The Two Goats Only One Offering, - - - - 190
III. ENTRANCE OF THE HIGH PRIEST INTO THE MOST HOLY PLACE, - - - - - - - - 191
IV. TRUTHS TAUGHT AND SYMBOLIZED BY THE DAY OF ATONEMENT, - - - - - - - 193
   1. The Value of the Sin-Sacrifice, - - - - - 194
   2. Expiation of Sin, - - - - - - - - 194
      (1) The Word "Atonement" Employed, - - 195
      (2) "Atonement" Means a "Covering," - - 195
      (3) The Blood of the Sacrificial Lamb the Means of Effecting Atonement, - - - 197
      (4) The Atonement Vicarious, - - - - 197
      (5) The Idea of Expiation, Propitiation, Included in Atonement, - - - 198
   3. The Prominence of the Blood of Expiation, - - 199
   4. The Action of the High Priest Typical of Christ, 200
   5. The Day a Graphic Picture of Christ's Work of Atonement, - - - - - - - 202
SUMMARY, - - - - - - - - - - - - 203

CHAPTER VI

THE SACRED FEASTS

NUMBER AND NAMES OF THE FEASTS, - - - - - - 207
I. THE SABBATH, - - - - - - - - - - 208
II. THE PASSOVER, - - - - - - - - - - 211
III. THE FEAST OF FIRST-FRUITS, - - - - - - 215

CONTENTS

	PAGE
IV. PENTECOST,	217
V. THE FEAST OF TRUMPETS,	222
VI. THE DAY OF ATONEMENT—THE YEAR OF JUBILEE,	228
1. The Term "Jubilee,"	230
2. The Beginning of the Jubilee,	230
3. The Jubilee Brought Rest to the Land,	230
4. The Privileges and Immunities of the Jubilee,	232
VII. THE FEAST OF TABERNACLES,	236
1. A Hebrew Thanksgiving,	237
2. The Most Joyous of the Festivals,	237
3. A Commemoration of Tent Life in the Wilderness,	238
4. The Sacrifices Offered,	239
CONCLUDING REMARKS,	240
INDEX,	243

ILLUSTRATIONS

The Tabernacle according to Fergusson, - - *Frontispiece*

OPPOSITE PAGE

The Tabernacle according to Brown, - - - - - 31

Ground Plan of the Tabernacle, - - - - - - 40

The Brazen Altar, - - - - - - - - - 41

The Laver, - - - - - - - - - - - 48

The Candlestick, - - - - - - - - - 56

The Table of Showbread, - - - - - - - 62

The Golden Altar of Incense, - - - - - - 66

The Ark of the Covenant, - - - - - - - 75

High Priest, - - - - - - - - - - - 91

STUDIES IN THE MOSAIC INSTITUTIONS

CHAPTER I

INTRODUCTION

THE GOSPEL IN THE OLD TESTAMENT

"THE figure was made by the truth and the truth was recognized by the figure. . . . Jesus Christ, whom both Testaments regard, the Old as its expectation, the New as its exemplar, both as their center."—*Pascal*.

*Novum Testamentum in Vetere latet:
Vetus Testamentum in Novo patet.*—*Augustine*.

"The New Testament in the Old is concealed;
The Old Testament in the New is revealed."

THE gospel of the grace of God was as certainly preached by Moses as by Isaiah or Ezekiel. In the tabernacle of the wilderness, in the preisthood and sacrifices, the same fundamental doctrines of reconciliation with God, of access to him and communion with him, are found in type and symbol as are revealed in the Gospels and the Epistles. The New Testament is the guaranty for our belief in the typical element in the Old.

Jesus said, "For had ye believed Moses, ye would have believed me: for he wrote of me" (John 5 : 46); "These are the words which I spake unto you, while I was yet with you, that all things must be fulfilled which were written in the law of Moses, and in the Prophets, and in the Psalms, concerning me" (Luke 24 : 44). In the twenty-seventh verse of Luke 24 we read, "And beginning at Moses and all the Prophets, he expounded unto them in all the scriptures the things concerning himself." The Lord Jesus, after his resurrection and shortly before his ascension into glory, most solemnly affirmed and testified that he himself is the center and subject of the Old Testament Scriptures and of every part of them. The testimony of Paul is as explicit as that of Jesus. To the chief men of the Jewish colony at Rome he "expounded and testified the kingdom of God, persuading them concerning Jesus, both out of the law of Moses, and out of the Prophets, from morning till evening" (Acts 28 : 23). The Son of God and his greatest apostle alike found in the law of Moses, in the rites and offices instituted by Moses, no less than in the Prophets, abundant proof of the person, work, and glory of the promised Deliverer. With Christ and his apostles the economy of Moses was instinct with preintimations of the Messiah. They saw in it the foregleams of our glorious dispensation, and of the coming glory. Moses preached the gospel.

Various terms are employed by the New Testament writers to designate this typical element. They speak of the Mosaic institutions as being a *shadow* (σκιά) of things to come (Col. 2 : 17; Heb. 10 : 1), as if the substance or reality that was still future had cast its shadow forward into the old economy. "Shadow" implies both dimness and transitoriness; but it implies also that there was a measure of resemblance between the one and the other. The apostle adds, "The body is of Christ"; that is, Christ is the reality and realization of Judaism as a system. Another term is *parable* (παραβολή) (Heb. 9 : 9); the tabernacle and its services formed an *illustration, outline,* or *figure* for "the time then present." A third term is *type* (τύπος), the image or representation of something yet future. Of the priests in Israel we read, "Who serve unto the example and shadow of heavenly things, as Moses was admonished of God when he was about to make the tabernacle : for, See, saith he, that thou make all things according to the *pattern* [type] showed to thee in the mount" (Heb. 8 : 5). This quotation from Exodus 25 : 40 is introduced to confirm the apostle's statement, that the tabernacle and the priesthood of Israel were adumbrations of heavenly realities. What are we to understand by this pattern or *type* exhibited to Moses? Was it a visible model? Was it a drawing? Or was it something presented to his mind in a vision? We cannot tell. But this much is surely a legitimate inference from the language: that Moses modeled the earthly sanctuary according to the supernatural view presented to him in the mount; that it was designed and fitted to be a type or copy of heavenly things; and that the priestly functions connected with it related to the same exalted truths. The whole constituted a picture or object-lesson for the instruction of the Lord's people. Hence no liberty was allowed Moses in making it. His orders were to adhere strictly to the pattern showed him. Any deviation from it would have marred the type, and incurred the Lord's displeasure. Man's genius and art had no play or part either in the plan or the purpose. Even Bezaleel, the chief craftsman, was inspired for his work (Ex. 31 : 1-5). Yet the prescriptions were so strict and precise that there was no room for the display of invention or taste.

Furthermore, we are told that "Christ is not entered into the holy places made with hands, which are the figures of the true; but into heaven itself, now to appear in the presence of God for us" (Heb. 9: 24). Noteworthy is the word rendered "figures" in this verse — *antitypes*, "outlines," "like in pattern" (R.V.); and its meaning here is the exact opposite of that commonly attaching to it. Here it signifies *foretypes;* that is, types instituted beforehand to prefigure the glorious Archetype. The earthly sanctuary reflected the heavenly. There is an analogy between the one and the other, between the way of reaching the sacred shrine of the one and of entering into the ineffable glory of the other. As Aaron passed from the altar of sacrifice into the most holy place and sprinkled the blood on the mercy-seat, thus completing the propitiation for the sins of the people, so Christ has entered into heaven itself, having by his own blood obtained eternal redemption for us. The first is the foretype of the second. In the divine economy the two stand related as promise and realization, as prediction and fulfillment. According to this profound verse, therefore, the great doctrine of redemption by the blood of Christ was in the ceremonial law, veiled indeed, but not altogether concealed. As a Puritan expressed it, it was hidden therein, yet shining ("et latet et lucet").

A fourth term is *pattern, copy* ($\dot{\upsilon}\pi\acute{o}\delta\varepsilon\iota\gamma\mu a$), a word which ordinarily exhibits to the eye the sketch or image of something that is invisible. Thus we read in Hebrews 9: 23, "It was therefore necessary that the patterns of things in the heavens should be purified with these; but the heavenly things themselves with better sacrifices than these." The term "patterns" in this verse represents the Greek word cited above, and it is rendered "copies" in the Revision. It is here affirmed that the priests serve the copies, sketches, or delineations of the heavenly things. But these copies are the tabernacle and its complex rites, and they are closely connected with the heavenly realities; they exist by virtue of the realities. The conclusion is unmistakable: the earthly sanctuary, the priesthood and their services, were all types, and only types. The religious system established through the agency of Moses was not an end in itself; it was the pledge and promise of our great High Priest, Jesus Christ, and of the eternal sanctuary of which he is Minister. The value of it all lies in this, that it was a picture drawn by the hand of God himself of the plan of salvation. Accordingly, it was perfectly adapted to the purposes for which it was appointed, but it was temporary and preparatory. Dawn is not day, though the two are inseparably connected. The Old Testament saints had light, but it was reflected light, for the Sun of Righteousness was not yet risen. The true Light now shines. But it is the same light then and now,—then seen as in a glass darkly, now blazing with undimmed splendor. The Mosaic institutions are a prophecy of the Lord Jesus Christ and of the redemption we have in him.

But the evidence is not yet all in. The terms which the inspired writers employ to describe the typical element in ancient Judaism, rich and suggestive as these terms are, do not exhaust the divine testimony on the subject. Far more than this is furnished us in the scriptures of the New Testament. We turn to another line of evidence which to an old-fashioned believer in the supreme authority of the Bible settles the question as to the predictive character of the Mosaic institutions.

Two ordinances lie at the foundation of Israel's relation to God as the covenant nation—the Passover and the Day of Expiation. The national history began with the Passover and the exodus. All subsequent legislation assumes the national existence, and rests on the two prime facts of redemption and deliverance. But what is the deepest significance of the paschal lamb, of which not a bone was to be broken? "For even Christ our passover is sacrificed for us," is Paul's answer. Majestic was the ritual of the Day of Atonement, when Aaron passed beyond the veil into the most holy place, and, standing before the awful Presence at the ark, sprinkled the blood of the sin-offering on the mercy-seat. But had this solemn transaction, the most sacred of all the Mosaic rites, no ulterior object—no higher aim than to cover *ceremonially* the sins of the congregation—than to effect a sort of scenic expiation? Let Romans 3 : 25 answer: "Whom God hath set forth to be a propitiation [a mercy-seat] through faith in his blood, to declare his righteousness for the remission of sins that are past, through the forbearance of God." Let Hebrews 9 : 7-12 also make the conclusive answer: "But into the second went the high priest alone once every year, not without blood, which he offered for himself, and for the errors of the people: the Holy Ghost this signifying, that the way into the holiest of all was not yet made manifest, while as the first tabernacle was yet standing: which was a figure for the time then present, in which were offered both gifts and sacrifices, that could not make him that did the service perfect, as pertaining to the conscience; which stood only in meats and drinks, and divers washings, and carnal ordinances, imposed on them until the time of reformation. But Christ being come an High Priest of good things to come, by a greater and more perfect tabernacle, not made with hands, that is to say, not of this building; neither by the blood of goats and calves, but by his own blood he entered in once into the holy place, having obtained eternal redemption for us." Here is both contrast and comparison: two holy places, two sacrifices, two entrances with blood, two priests, two expiations. The one was Aaron, the other Christ; the one was the blood of a sacrificial beast, the other was his own blood; the one was the earthly sanctuary, the other the heavenly; the one was a symbol, the other its reality; the one was picture, the other its original; the one was the prediction, the other its fulfillment. We may summarize it all thus: *Israel's day of atonement perfected in the person and work of the Lord Jesus Christ.*

While both these ordinances, the Passover and the annual Expiation, were intended to effect, and they did effect, a positive good during the time of their observance by Israel, yet this by no means exhausts the divine intention in their institution. They were filled with a noble prophecy; they looked forward to a blessed future; and the Holy Spirit in the New Testament has knit together the prediction and its accomplishment.

In the discussion hitherto conducted we have had frequent occasion to refer to the Epistle to the Hebrews. We turn to it now to study its general bearing on the question of the typical character of the Mosaic institutions.

The epistle is an inspired commentary on ancient Judaism. All the prominent features of that system are graphically reviewed by the writer, and at his touch each of them becomes instinct with life, and glows with a profound meaning. The thoughts spring from the heart of the Old Testament. The language is largely drawn from the books of Moses. The imagery is taken bodily from the tabernacle, the priesthood, the altar, and sacrifices of Israel. The doctrinal portion of the epistle (chs. 1–10) falls into two main divisions. The theme of the first division is, Jesus our High Priest (chs. 1–7). The theme of the second is, The Offering of Our High Priest, Himself (chs. 8–10). Even the exhortations with which it abounds are based on events in the history of the Hebrew people. The first is found in chapter 2 : 1-4, and it is based on the scenes connected with the giving of the law at Sinai. The second exhortation is chapter 3 : 7–4 : 5, and its powerful appeal is grounded upon the wilderness journey. The third is chapter 4 : 6-16, and has for its background the rest of Canaan. The fourth is chapter 10 : 19-31, and here the tremendous appeal is drawn from the temple and its sprinkled blood. The last exhortation is chapter 12 : 18-29, and it is taken, as to its metaphors, from the holy city, Jerusalem. This very brief and compressed analysis will serve to show how closely Hebrews is interwoven with the history and worship of Israel.

But there is much more in this precious scripture. The Spirit is here constantly finding the germs of the New Testament dispensation in the rites and ceremonies of Moses. Under his handling, "shell and husk, in which the precious kernel is hidden, fall away one after another until at length the kernel itself, the Christ, appears personally."[1]

History gives Melchizedek a very small niche (Gen. 14: 18-20; Ps. 110: 4). Hebrews 7 draws out at length the striking parallelism between the priesthood of Melchizedek and of Christ. The summing up of the argument is in verse 21: "The Lord sware and will not repent, Thou art a Priest for ever after the order of Melchisedec." Instantly at the touch of this verse Melchizedek becomes transparent, and a greater Priest is seen through him; he almost disappears in the person of the Messiah.

Aaron and his successors stood at the head of the priestly office in Israel. But those high priests were compassed with infirmity (5: 2); they must needs offer sacrifices for their own sins (5: 3); and they were not suffered to continue in the office by reason of death (7: 23). But the

[1] Herder.

Lord Jesus Christ, who is the perfect embodiment of all priestly types, has an unchangeable priesthood because he continues forever, and he is holy, undefiled, and undefilable (7 : 24, 26). The whole Levitical order now disappears, for it has found in him its realization and its completion.

The sacrifices offered under the law could not take away sins; and so they must be multiplied. Day by day and year after year fresh victims must bleed; the altar was always wet with blood, and the smoke of the holocaust ever ascended (10 : 1-4). But Christ "now once in the end of the world hath appeared to put away sin by the sacrifice of himself" (9 : 26). "But this man, after he had offered one sacrifice for sins for ever, sat down on the right hand of God" (10 : 12). The Levitical offerings were only shadows cast before of that one perfect offering which in due time our blessed Lord was to present to God whereby all believers were to receive remission of sins; but the two offerings—that under the law, this by Christ—are bound together as type and antitype, as picture and reality.

Priestly ministry under the law related to the ritual service of the earthly sanctuary (9 : 6-9). "We have such an High Priest, who is set on the right hand of the throne of the Majesty in the heavens; a minister of the sanctuary, and of the true tabernacle, which the Lord pitched, and not man" (8: 1, 2). Christ is here declared to be the minister of "the true tabernacle." The word "true" (ἀληθινῆς) must not be taken in the sense of opposition to what is false. There is another Greek term that expresses this idea (ἀληθής). The earthly sanctuary was not a lie. The word here employed signifies, not antagonism, but contrast. It answers to the perfect ideal; it stands opposed to all more or less imperfect representations. It means real and genuine, as distinguished from what is temporary and symbolical. "The true tabernacle" is the heaven of glory,[1] and *it* is the perfect and eternal realization of all that the wilderness tent foreshadowed, just as the "true bread from heaven" is the veritable food of the soul, of which the manna was no more than a symbol. The manna was bread, though not the true bread. Christ alone is that. The heavenly sanctuary is the everlasting original, of which the earthly was no more than a dim and distant copy. But the one corresponds to the other as shadow and substance, as type and antitype.

The covenant of Sinai by which the Hebrew people were constituted into the theocracy was but the harbinger of the new covenant (8: 6-13). The promises of the old covenant contemplated,

[1] Delitzsch.

for the most part, earthly privileges and blessings, as the possession of the land, and the enjoyment of the divine protection and favor, so long as the people remained obedient. But it was temporary and preparatory. The new covenant rests on three "better" things—a better ministry, better covenant (that is, better in its terms and provisions), and better promises. The old could boast of nothing more than the symbol of the divine presence; this secures the abiding indwelling of the Spirit in God's people.

The rest of Canaan was but a figure of the better rest, the true sabbath-keeping, which remains for the people of God (ch. 4).

The earthly Jerusalem was but an imperfect image of the heavenly city, and the congregation but a dim reflection of the "general assembly and church of the firstborn who are enrolled in heaven" (12: 18-23, R. V.).

The marvelous correspondence between Judaism and Christianity, as it is developed in the Epistle to the Hebrews, is neither accidental nor fortuitous. God is the author of both, therefore the remarkable connection between them. But Judaism was fashioned to prefigure Christianity, not the latter the former. The antitype is not constructed to resemble the type, but the type is constructed to bear the likeness of the antitype.

It is because of the antitype that the type exists. The Mosaic economy, being a rough draft of Christianity, presupposed its existence. Had Judaism been an end in itself, had it terminated in present observance, it could not have been the subject of apostolic exposition. But the New Testament writers do treat it as a prophetic system, as holding in itself the germs of future and more glorious revelations of the grace of God. They do treat it as a system which both showed and foreshowed. Therefore they fatally err who regard Judaism as the natural expression of the religious sentiment common to mankind, and who would class it with the various ethnic religions which have prevailed. No less do they err who refuse to see in it any prophetic or dispensational truth. They have read the New Testament to no purpose who thus treat the Mosaic institutions.

It should be remembered that the knowledge or the ignorance of the Old Testament worshipers touching the truth embodied in the ordinances which they observed is not the standard by which our intelligence of them is to be regulated. The typical teaching was intended indeed for them, but also for us, and it is profitable for us perhaps even more than it was for those ancient worthies. Scripture belongs to all God's people, and to all time. There is a manifoldness and comprehensiveness in it that no other writing possesses. The Spirit of God often combines a variety of ends and aims in what he is pleased to communicate. That others were in view when Judaism was established, is clear from Paul's words, "Now all these things happened unto them for ensamples [types]: and they are written for our admonition, upon whom the ends of the world are come" (I. Cor. 10 : 11). The ways of God with his people in the various world periods that are past reproduce themselves in the gospel age: the light that shone then shines now, only with the added glory of our dispensation: all gathers into the present time; all now instructs with a clearness and power that could not be known then. The Old Testament saints had no more than the rudimentary sketch, the dim outline. But it was enough for their guidance and faith, for it was divinely planned. Through that system there was presented to their faith the Lamb slain from the foundation of the world. The eye of faith might, as it gazed on the gorgeous ceremonies and followed the splendid ritual, be able to fill in the picture, and see in the distant future the great High Priest, who was promised, offering the most costly victim, himself; an altar consecrated by blood precious beyond all parallel, his own blood. Jesus said that Abraham saw his day and was glad (John 8:56). A fuller light was given through Moses than Abraham enjoyed, and it is quite possible that not a few clear-eyed saints read much of the gospel of God's grace as it shone through the skillfully carved lattice-work of their ordinances.

For Judaism had a voice for the chosen people, and its voice was prophetic. Its voice was the significant word *Wait*. Wait, and the true Priest will come, the Priest greater than Aaron, than Melchizedek. Wait, and the Prophet like unto Moses, but far greater than Moses, will appear. Wait, and the true Sacrifice, that of which all other offerings were but faint pictures, will be presented and sin be put away.

Weighty are the words of one equally eminent for his piety as for his learning: "God has been pleased to give, as well in remarkable persons of the Old Testament, in whose case something unusual occurred, as in the whole institution of religion, a true delineation—and one worthy of so great an artist—of Christ, together with his spiritual body."[1] As weighty are the words of another: "That the Old Testament is rich in types, or rather forms in its totality *one* type, of the New Testament, follows necessarily from the entirely unique position which belongs to Christ

[1] Witsius.

as the center of the history of the world and of revelation. As we constantly see the principle embodied in the vegetable and animal kingdoms, that the higher species are already typified in a lower stage of development, so do we find, in the domain of saving revelation, the highest not only prepared for, but also shadowed forth, by that which precedes in the lower spheres."[1] The words of a Greek writer (quoted by Taylor) we may venture to translate: "For what is the law? It is the gospel proclaimed beforehand. And what is the gospel? The law fulfilled."

To refuse to recognize any relation between Judaism and Christianity, as some now pretend to do; to regard the world periods and economies of the past as altogether dissevered from the present age, is to deny the unity of Scripture and of God's plan of redemption,—is to negate the witness of the New Testament, and to deprive us of a legacy which God surely meant should enrich our Christian thought.

The following studies in the Tabernacle, Priesthood, Sacrifices, and Feasts of ancient Israel have one aim, and only one, to wit: to show, however feebly, that the Mosaic institutions were planned and designed to teach the way of salvation, and to reveal Christ as God's appointed Prophet, Priest, and King.

[1] Van Oosterzee.

THE TABERNACLE ACCORDING TO BROWN.

CHAPTER II

THE TABERNACLE OF THE WILDERNESS

I. THE CONDITIONS OF WORSHIP

ORGANIZED worship implies a recognized body of worshipers. From the beginning God had his witnesses in the world. In the family of Abraham he formed his servants into a corporate body, and gave them a perfect system of worship—perfect for the ends for which it was established. The government under which Israel was placed was a theocracy. God was their King, and the twelve tribes formed the priestly kingdom (Ex. 19 : 6). One of the tribes, Levi, was set apart to the special service of Jehovah; one family of this tribe, Aaron's, was chosen the priestly family of the nation, and charged with the duties and functions of the priesthood (Ex. 28 : 1; Lev. 8; Num. 3 : 10). The priest was to minister before the Lord in behalf of the congregation (Ex. 28 : 1; Heb. 5 : 1), and to interpret and teach the law to the people (Lev. 10 : 8-11; Neh. 8 : 2, 8).

By reason of its sinfulness the congregation

could draw near to Jehovah only on the ground of an adequate atonement. This supreme want was provided for by a series of *sacrifices*, which were offered to God through the mediating agency of the priesthood (Lev. 1–7). A sacred *calendar* was also provided, which designated the times and seasons when the chosen people in a more solemn manner recognized their covenant relations with the Lord (Lev. 23, 25). One other appointment completed the organization of Israel as a corporate witness of the Lord in the earth, namely, a *central place of worship*. This the tabernacle was until it gave place to the more permanent house of the Lord, the temple at Jerusalem.

In the theocratic organization of Israel, accordingly, four features are made very prominent: the *place* of worship, the *ministry* of worship, the *means* of worship, the *times* of worship. A brief scriptural study of these essential parts of ancient Judaism is the object of the present writing. We begin with the Tabernacle.

The tabernacle was the first sanctuary built for God at his own command, and it was rendered forever illustrious by his indwelling presence. A dozen chapters of the Pentateuch are devoted to a description of its structure and contents,—hardly two to the record of the creation of the world.

Its pattern and the instructions relating to its complicated services were directly communicated to Moses by Jehovah. The materials required for its construction were the gifts of a willing-hearted people.

The tabernacle and the system of ordinances of which it was the center, was, and was designed to be, an adumbration or prefiguration of greater and better things to be enjoyed in the dispensation of the grace of God under the gospel. In Hebrews 9 : 9 the inspired writer describes it and its services as a " figure for the time then present" — rather, a *parable* ($παραβολή$). It was an acted parable, designed to instruct the Old Testament saints in God's plan of redemption. In a shadowy form it foretold the blessings and benefits to be brought to the world by the advent of the Messiah. It preached the gospel. It was a divine object-lesson, an embodied prophecy of good things to come, a witness to the grace and saving power of Him who had devised and was now revealing his way of bringing sinners to himself. It taught salvation through propitiation, forgiveness through bloodshedding. Access to God and worship it disclosed. The holiness of God, the sinfulness of man, and the reconciliation which in due time should be effected, are all clearly set forth by the tabernacle and its rites.

Much of the language of the New Testament is drawn from this ancient sanctuary and its ordinances. "Mercy-seat," "propitiation," "veil," "washing of regeneration," "high priest," "redemption," "intercession," "cleansed," "purged," "sacrifice," "offering," "access to God," "drawing near to God," etc., are words and phrases that either have arisen from or are illustrated by the tabernacle and its ceremonies. The doctrine of substitution, central in the Christian system, is elucidated in the rites of ancient Judaism with a clearness which perhaps is not surpassed in any other portion of the Bible.

II. THE NAMES OF THE TABERNACLE.

Three principal titles are given to the tabernacle. The first is *tent* (*ohel*) (Ex. 26:36). Those who have examined the word closely (Gesenius, Cook, Plumptre), are of the opinion that it denotes the outer coverings; namely, the curtain of goats' hair, the rams' skins dyed red, and the "badgers' skins." Granting this general application of the term, it would be precarious to build on this uncertain foundation the imaginary structure which Mr. Fergusson, the British architect, has contrived and pictured for us in Smith's Dictionary of the Bible (Article "Temple"); namely, an outer tent with a ridge-pole, beneath which the tabernacle proper was housed. Those who have profoundly studied the subject, as Soltau and W. Brown, are persuaded that the plan of the London architect is wide of the mark.

The second name is *tabernacle* (*mishkan*) (Ex. 25 : 9), a word which Plumptre derives from one that means to *settle down, to dwell;* hence, a dwelling. This title seems to be used in a somewhat indefinite way; for example, for the curtains, for the frame-work of boards, and for the entire structure. Generally, however, it designates the sacred dwelling of the Lord with all its belongings. These two names are sometimes found joined together, as in Exodus 40 : 2, 6, 29: "the tabernacle of the tent of meeting" (R.V.).

The third name is *sanctuary* (Ex. 25 : 8 : "And let them make me a sanctuary") (*mikdash*), a name, we are told, never applied to the temple of heathen deities. It denotes especially the holiness of the place of worship, the dwelling of Him who is infinitely holy, and who can tolerate no evil.

Other descriptive titles are given the sanctuary, two of which deserve a brief notice. In the so-called Authorized Version of the Scripture we often find this expression: "the tabernacle of the congregation" (Ex. 29 : 42, 44, ff.)—a somewhat misleading translation, for it seems to indicate the place of meeting for the children of Israel. The Revised Version renders it, "the tent of meeting"; that is, the place of meeting between God and the people—"where I will meet with you, to speak there unto thee. And there I will meet with the children of Israel" (Ex. 29 : 42, 43). It was at the tabernacle, with its priesthood and sacrifices, that God met with his chosen people, the only place where he could meet with sinners —the place of propitiation and reconciliation.

In Numbers 1 : 50, 53, another descriptive title is found : "the tabernacle of testimony." Oehler is of the opinion that this phrase designates the sanctuary as the place of revelation. Certainly God did declare his will there, but he specially testified to them by his holy Law, which within the ark witnessed to the covenant engagements they had assumed at Sinai, and against their sins.

III. DESCRIPTION OF THE TABERNACLE.

The tabernacle was a rectangular structure, thirty cubits long and ten wide. The cubit is reckoned at eighteen inches. It was the measure of a man's arm from the elbow to the tip of the middle finger.[1] Accordingly, it was forty-five feet in length, fifteen wide, and fifteen high. It

[1] Fergusson.

was divided into two rooms, or compartments, the first being the Holy Place, which contained the Candlestick, Table of Showbread, and Altar of Incense. Behind it was the Most Holy Place, a cube in form, being ten cubits every way. The only object in the Holy of Holies was the Ark of the Covenant. This room was the Shrine, the dwelling-place of the God of Israel, therefore called "the Holiest of all" (Heb. 9:3). The two rooms were separated by a gorgeous hanging or veil of fine twined linen in blue, purple, and scarlet, and inwrought with cherubic figures.

The frame of the tabernacle was constructed out of boards of acacia ("shittim") wood, a species of locust or thorn with which the Peninsula of Sinai abounds. The Septuagint translates the word "shittim" into "incorruptible wood," probably because it was of a solid and durable fiber. There were forty-eight such boards, each furnished with two tenons that fitted into two corresponding sockets of silver. The Israelites contributed one hundred talents of silver for these sockets (Ex. 38:25-28), and it is described as atonement money (Ex. 30:16). So this portable temple rested on silver, which the people paid as their ransom. It was a costly foundation, for about two hundred thousand dollars went into it. Besides, the boards of the framework were overlaid with gold, and gold entered largely into the construction of all the furniture of the tabernacle. Kitto's estimate of its cost is one million two hundred and fifty thousand dollars; that of W. Brown, one million five hundred thousand dollars.

Ten magnificent curtains, wrought of fine linen and beautified with royal colors of blue, purple, and scarlet, interwoven with cherubim in the most skillful manner, formed the ceiling. Three outer coverings of goats' hair, rams' skins dyed red, and badgers' skins were provided to protect it from the inclemency of the weather. From these exterior covers the name of "tent" seems to be derived. The Revisers have changed "badgers' skins" into "sealskins," and in the margin "porpoise-skins" is given as an alternate rendering. Whatever animal is meant by the term, whether of the land or the sea, it was likely a large creature. Sandals were made out of the same skins (Ezek. 16 : 10 : "I have shod thee with badgers' skin"). Is it possible that the shoes which the Israelites wore during the long wilderness journey, and which so effectively protected them that their feet "did not swell," were made of these skins?

IV. THE POSITION OF THE TABERNACLE.

The tabernacle occupied a central place among the tribes. Whether in the camp or on the march, it was always in the center. The encampment was in the form of a hollow square, with three tribes stationed on each of its four sides. The sacred tent was pitched in the center of this square, with its door always facing the east. On the side opposite, to the eastward, was the division of Judah, with 186,000 men of arms. On the south was the division of Reuben, which numbered 151,450 men of war. On the west was the division of Ephraim, 108,100 strong. On the north was the division of Dan, 157,600 strong. The men of war comprising these four grand divisions of Israel's army numbered 603,550. (Num. 1.) Each division had its own appropriate standard, each tribe and family its own ensign. It is impossible to determine what the standards were. Canon Cook infers from the significance of the name (*to glitter, to shine afar*), that it was a solid figure mounted on a pole, "such as the Egyptians used," which is no more than a guess. Tradition alleges that the standards represented the cherubim—the lion, man, ox, and eagle, but there exists no means of verifying it. Within the space enclosed by the camp the tabernacle stood, and the tribes faced it on the four sides of the square. Just what the distance was from it to each division cannot be determined; perhaps about a mile. At any rate, the tent was in the center of Israel in the encampment.

In the journeys of the wilderness the tabernacle held a similar central position. When the pillar of cloud gave the signal to march (Num. 9:17), Judah was the first to strike his tents and set forth. Then the frame-work and coverings of the tabernacle, in charge of the sons of Gershon and Merari, followed (Num. 10:17). The second division, that of Reuben, marched next; and the sanctuary, in charge of the Kohathites, followed (Num. 10:21). The other two divisions marched after the sanctuary, that of Dan bringing up the rear. Thus the tabernacle was again in the center, six tribes being in the van and six in the rear. "God is in the midst of her; she shall not be moved: God shall help her, and that right early" (Ps. 46:5). How forcible this language becomes when we remember the central position of the tent of meeting.

V. THE COURT AND ITS CONTENTS.

A distinguishing feature of the sanctuary was the Court that surrounded it. This court, or enclosure, was a double square, one hundred cubits long and fifty broad. It was formed by pillars or graceful columns standing upright in sockets of brass, the spaces between being

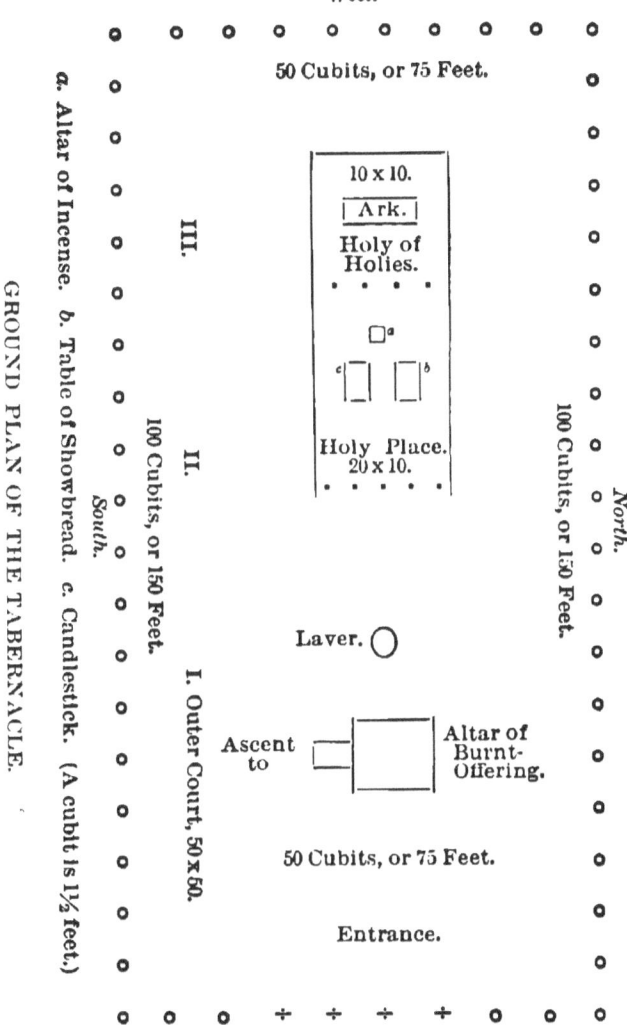

GROUND PLAN OF THE TABERNACLE.

a. Altar of Incense. b. Table of Showbread. c. Candlestick. (A cubit is 1½ feet.)

FROM MOTEL. THE BRAZEN ALTAR. Scale—½ inch to cubit.

filled by hangings of fine twined linen (Ex. 27 : 9-18). At the east end was the gateway, twenty cubits wide and guarded by an immense screen of fine twined linen in blue, purple, and scarlet. Within this enclosure the Levites and the priests were stationed. The Levites, in three divisions (named after the three sons of Levi), occupied the northern, southern, and western sides, while the priests held the place of honor, the east end of the court opposite the door of the sanctuary.

Between the door of the court and the door of the tabernacle stood two objects of great interest. The first was the Altar of Burnt-Offering; the second was the Laver.

1. *The Brazen Altar.*
(Ex. 27: 1-8; 38: 1-7.)

The altar of sacrifice was a conspicuous part of the Mosaic system. All priestly ministry and every act of worship were connected with it. If the individual Israelite or the congregation in its corporate capacity sought to draw near to God, the altar was the one indispensable means. It is hardly too much to say that the life of Israel as a nation, and the life of each member of the nation, was in some important respects bound up with the altar. The Scriptures designate it in three ways: First, it is called simply "the altar"

(Ex. 27 : 1, R.V.), a name which expresses the idea of sacrifice, for the Hebrew term is derived from one meaning *to kill* or *slay*. The *altar* signifies preëminently bloodshedding, expiation. Second, "the altar of the burnt offering" (Lev. 4 : 7, 10, 18). It was thus named, doubtless, because of the prominence of the burnt-offering in the Levitical system. A deeper thought, however, seems to lie in the name. The word *burnt-offering* denotes that which ascends; and it is applied to the altar because what was consumed upon it was given up to God, and ascended to him, and was for his satisfaction. Third, "Thou shalt set the altar of burnt offering before the door of the tabernacle of the tent of meeting" (Ex. 40 : 6, R.V.). This verse designates neither a new nor a different name nor a function of the altar. It designates its position before the tabernacle door, and emphasizes the truth that propitiation for sins precedes entrance into God's presence. It was the one way, the only one, of access to God in the sanctuary. It signified that a door of entrance was provided, that all who came by it would be accepted; but it forbade the notion that any other way of approach to God could be had.

(1) *Its Form.* The altar was square, five cubits in length and breadth by three cubits in height; hollow, without a covering and without a

bottom. The frame was of acacia, overlaid with heavy plates of brass; hence it is sometimes called "the brasen altar" (Ex. 38 : 30). The corners or angle-posts projected above the upper surface, and were fashioned into *horns*. Dr. Murphy thinks that the height of the altar was measured from the top of the horns to the bottom, not from the table or upper plane.[1] The priests, accordingly, could perform their functions at the altar with convenience while standing on the ground.

Considerable difference of opinion exists as to the "compass," and the "grate of network of brass" (Ex. 27 : 4, 5). Some hold that the "compass," or "ledge" (R.V.), was a sort of shelf or platform running round the altar on the outside and midway its height, and the grate was the support of this platform, parallel with its edge and reaching to the ground. Others think the "compass" was a cincture or band at the top for ornamentation, as the ark, table, and altar of incense had borders or crowns; that it reached down to the grate, which was placed in the interior, and on which the sacrifices were burnt. The rings by which it was borne cut through the angles of the altar and caught into the corners of the grate and held it firm. This last view is favored by the Septuagint Version so far as the

[1] See Commentary *in loc.*

"grate" is concerned, which it renders "hearth" or "fireplace" (ἐσχάρα). We are inclined to the latter view; namely, that the grate of network of brass was set in the interior of the altar.

If the grate was inside and midway its height, then the mercy-seat and the grate were exactly on a level. Mercy and expiation are coördinate; forgiveness and atonement are coextensive; "without shedding of blood is no remission." Moreover, the table of showbread was of the same height as the mercy-seat and the brazen grate of the altar —a fact that seems to symbolize that communion with God is grounded in atonement. Pardon, reconciliation, and fellowship with God depend on the Blood!

(2) *The Horns of the Altar.* These were of a piece with the altar itself, not separate attachments of it (Ex. 38: 2). "Horns were not usual adjuncts of altars; indeed, they seem to have been peculiar to those of the Israelites."[1] One use of them is clearly indicated in Psalm 118: 27: "Bind the sacrifice with cords, even unto the horns of the altar." If it was the living animal that was thus confined, the horns must have been of great strength and firmness. Perhaps it is from this fact that the idea of power and might, so often in Scripture connected with

[1] Rawlinson.

horns, is derived. "The horns were symbolical of power, protection, and help; and at the same time, of glory and salvation."[1] This statement is justified by such passages as I. Samuel 2: 1, 10; II. Samuel 22: 3; Psalm 89: 17; 112: 9, etc. A certain inviolability attached to the altar's horns. He who laid hold upon them was regarded as safe, and enjoyed immunity, except in the case of criminality (I. Kings 1: 50; 2: 28). It is likely that this notion of sanctuary arose from the deep truth that salvation is associated in Scripture with the horns of the altar. Because of propitiation there made, the idea of immunity probably originated.

It is noteworthy that it was the blood of the sin-offering which was sprinkled on the horns of the brazen altar, and it was the same blood which was carried into the most holy place and sprinkled on the mercy-seat, and on the veil, and smeared on the horns of the golden altar (Ex. 29 : 12; 30 : 10; Lev. 4 : 7, etc.). From these and similar passages it is inferred that salvation was closely allied in the minds of God's people with the blood of expiation. The horns lifted up the blood of atonement, as it were, into the sight and presence of God—the blood without which no approach to him was possible.

[1] Kalisch.

(3) *The Position of the Altar.* "And thou shalt set the altar of burnt offering before the door of the tabernacle of the tent of meeting" (Ex. 40 : 6, R. V.). The expression seems to intimate that the altar directly faced the door of the sacred tent. But in point of fact it was nearer the gate of the court than the door of the tabernacle. The laver stood between it and the door of the latter (Ex. 40 : 30).

Its position was very significant. It was the first object which the approaching worshiper encountered on passing into the court. There was no drawing nigh the dwelling of the God of Israel without first going by the altar. Before the sinner can meet with God in peace and hold communion with him, he must be forgiven and accepted. The whole question of sin, as between him and God, must be divinely settled before any true fellowship with God can be enjoyed. At the altar of sacrifice that question was definitely and finally settled. The description of the tabernacle and its furniture starts with the holy of holies and moves outward to the court (Ex. 25–27). The order observed is the following: the ark, table, candlestick, frame and curtains, altar of sacrifice. God goes forth from his dwelling-place and meets the sinner at the altar. How can the holy and just God receive and forgive guilty man? No more tremendous problem could be propounded. In his infinite love and grace God himself answered the question in a way perfectly consistent with the demands of his righteousness and truth and man's supreme need. The *altar* is the answer to all Divine claims of law and justice on the one hand, and to the sinner's dire necessity on the other. ⌜There sin was punished in the person of a substitute; death, the penalty due sin, inflicted; satisfaction rendered to law and justice, and reconciliation effected; and the justified one may pass into the awful Presence, and worship God in peace and comfort.⌝

The altar stood at the door of entrance—this signifying, that access to God is had only through expiation. The position of the altar taught a mighty truth, a vital and fundamental lesson: namely, we draw nigh to God by the way of atonement, the blood-sprinkled way. Christ is the only way to the Father; "I am the way, and the truth, and the life: no man cometh unto the Father, but by me" (John 14:6). "I am the door: by me if any man enter in, he shall be saved, and shall go in and out, and find pasture" (John 10:9). "Neither is there salvation in any other: for there is none other name under heaven given among men whereby we must be saved" (Acts 4:12). ⌜No man, no matter how religious or devout, how generous and philanthropic, how strictly controlled by principles of rectitude in his relations with his fellow-men, how splendid his gifts and how varied his acquirements,—no man, no matter who or what he be, will ever enter the true heavenly tabernacle who refuses first to come to the Altar of Sacrifice.] Sin *must* be judged and blotted out before we can be admitted into fellowship with God, and into the holy society of heaven.

2. *The Laver.*
(Ex. 30 : 17-21 ; 38 : 8.)

(1) This important article was made out of the brass mirrors contributed by the women who assembled at the door of the tent of meeting (Ex. 38 : 8). The Revision describes them as "the serving women which served at the door," etc. Just what is meant by this statement it is not easy to determine. Probably they were devout women who loved the public services of Jehovah, and who manifested their devotion by their attendance on his worship. They may have been the same persons who spun the linen and the goats' hair needed for the construction of the tabernacle (Ex. 35 : 25, 26): the "wise-hearted" and devoted women. Certainly they were no *order*, or guild, like nuns or "sisters." Israel had no such order.

THE LAVER.

(2) *The form* of the laver is not described, but most likely it was of a roundish shape, and sufficiently large to contain all the water required for the priestly ablutions, and probably also for the washing of the parts of the burnt-offering (Lev. 1: 9). The basin rested on a base called the "foot." This is constantly mentioned; the phrase is, "the laver and his foot." The foot seems to have been something distinct from the body or bowl, and perhaps was separable. Some are of the opinion that the foot was a saucer-like basin, which received its supply of water, as needed, from the laver, which it supported by a shaft arising out of its center.

(3) The laver stood between the altar of sacrifice and the door of the tabernacle. There, every time the priests entered the sanctuary for any service, they were obliged to wash their hands and their feet. So strict was the injunction that death was the penalty for neglect. Twice these solemn words are used: "that they die not" (Ex. 30 : 20, 21).

(4) The laver sets forth typically *sanctification, holiness*. The psalmist alludes to its cleansing efficacy when he says, "I will wash mine hands in innocency: so will I compass thine altar" (Ps. 26 : 6 ; 73 : 13). Water is nature's great purifier.

All the world wash with water as well as quench their thirst. There is a solvent power in it which removes what is foul, and purifies what is polluted,—expressive type of that cleansing without which fellowship with God is impossible. The unwashed priest perished. God's holy presence demands nothing less. Complete and perfect purity alone is fitted to be near him. The priest drew nigh to God by the shedding of sacrificial blood at the altar, and by washing his hands and feet at the laver. His action was symbolical. We draw nigh to God through that of which both altar and laver were only shadows; namely, the atoning work of Christ and the regenerating power of the Holy Spirit. The priestly washings at the brazen laver have their antitype in all the means God has ordained for our sanctification; for example, the word, the ordinances, and especially in the gracious influences of the Holy Spirit.

The laver prefigures regeneration. In Titus 3 : 5 we read, "Not by works of righteousness which we have done, but according to his mercy he saved us, by the washing of regeneration, and renewing of the Holy Ghost." The phrase, "washing of regeneration," literally rendered, is, *laver of regeneration*. The Greek term is the same as that used by the Septuagint in Exodus 30 : 18.

The reference seems to be to the laver of the tabernacle. The renewing by the Spirit is a creative act, and is identical with being born again, or born anew. This regeneration is described as being by the laver, or washing by the Spirit. But what is the laver? Baptism? We think not. In Ephesians 5 : 25, 26, Paul tells us that "Christ also loved the church, and gave himself for it; that he might sanctify and cleanse it with the washing [laver, τῷ λουτρῷ] of water by the word." The word is here represented as achieving the results of the bath—cleansing, sanctifying. Is this the office of baptism? We certainly think not. The means the Holy Spirit employs to effect this radical and profound change in a sinner, which is called regeneration, is *the word, the truth of God*. James writes, "Of his own will begat he us with the word of truth" (Jas. 1 : 18). Peter writes, "Being born again, not of corruptible seed, but of incorruptible, by the word of God, which liveth and abideth for ever" (I. Pet. 1 : 23). This testimony is unmistakable and conclusive. The agent of regeneration is the Spirit; the instrument he employs in effecting it is the word of God; no ordinance, however important,—no rite, however precious, can ever effect it. This sheds light on John 3 : 5 : "Except a man be born of water and of the Spirit, he cannot enter into the kingdom of God." Surely the rite of baptism cannot here be meant, else would it become a necessary part of salvation, which it certainly is not. It is the *word* the Spirit employs in effecting the new birth. That the word is compared to water and its action, Ephesians 5 : 26 clearly proves: "that he might sanctify and cleanse it with the washing [laver] of water by the word." So also in John 15 : 3 Jesus says, "Now ye are clean through the word which I have spoken unto you." The word acts as a pruning-knife (John 15 : 1-5); as a sword (Heb. 4 : 12); a fire (Jer. 23 : 29); as water (I. Pet. 1 : 22). "The washing of regeneration" is an expression taken, not from baptism, but from the provision for priestly purification, the laver of the court.

The laver prefigures Christ's personal and abiding interest in his people. This truth, we conceive, is illustrated by the Lord's washing the disciples' feet (John 13 : 1-17). That act was designed to teach his followers the lesson of humility, of self-abnegation, and of reciprocal service and affection. Like his love for them was theirs to be for one another; his ran through all his ministry and association with them, and up to the very end of his earthly life: "Having loved his own which were in the world, he loved them unto the end." But did his love stop short at that point? Surely not. He would love them none the less when glorified — nay, all the more. To Peter he said, "He that is bathed needeth not save to wash his feet, but is clean every whit" (John 13:10, R. V.). There is a bath which requires no repetition, which is accomplished once for all. Regeneration is never repeated. A child of wrath, become a child of God, remains evermore God's child. Justified once, we are justified forever. Both acts, regeneration and justification, are simultaneous, instantaneous, complete, and final. "And such were some of you; but ye were washed, but ye were sanctified, but ye were justified in the name of the Lord Jesus Christ, and in the Spirit of our God" (I. Cor. 6:11, R. V.).

But the believer comes into daily contact with the world's defilement, and is polluted by his own remaining corruption. The old nature is still in him, although he is not in it, and constantly must he lament his failures, and confess his shortcomings. How is he to be kept clean? How is interrupted communion to be reëstablished? "If any man sin, we have an advocate with the Father, Jesus Christ the righteous" (I. John 2:1). By washing the disciples' feet he gave them and us the assurance and the pledge that on going to the Father's right hand he would not be unmindful of us who are left behind; he would undertake to keep us clean, and so meet for service here and glory hereafter.

The consecration of Aaron and his sons for the duties and the privileges of the priestly office serves to illustrate this point still further. First, they were washed, or bathed; next, Aaron was anointed; then the offerings were presented, and the sons were anointed with the holy oil and the blood. These acts were never repeated. The consecration was final and complete from the beginning. But each time they entered the sanctuary to perform the functions of their high office, they had to wash their hands and feet. No matter how often they entered the sacred precincts, every day and many times in a day they must wash. The provision for their purification was the brazen laver. Their consecration was at the altar; their cleansing at the laver. *Our* pardon, acceptance, and separation unto God are secured for us by the death of Christ. Our daily cleansing likewise through him is no less sure. Jesus prayed, "I pray not that thou shouldest take them out of the world, but that thou shouldest keep them from the evil." Christ is our Laver.

Two things are indispensable in order to glorify God and enjoy him forever: right relations with God and a right character in us. By right relations with God is meant a justified relation, a peace relation with him. By right character in ourselves is meant, deliverance from the dominion and the pollution of sin. Both believers have in Christ, and in him both are perfect. Both, too, are symbolized by the altar and laver in the court of the tabernacle. At the one, propitiation for sins is signified; at the other, purification from sins. At the one, justification is typified; at the other, sanctification, with regeneration as its initial step. At the altar, sin is judged and forgiven. At the laver, sin is washed away from the person. Jesus Christ in his atoning death and prevailing intercession is the glorious Antitype of both. Pardon, purity, power,—these are the stages.

VI. THE SANCTUARY AND ITS FURNITURE.

The sanctuary was a rectangular structure, forty-five feet in length by fifteen feet in width. It was divided into rooms, or compartments. The first was the Holy Place, thirty feet long; it contained the Candlestick, the Table of Showbread, and the Altar of Incense. Gold predominated in the sanctuary. All the sacred vessels were either wholly made of it, as the candlestick, the mercy-seat, and cherubim, or overlaid with the precious metal, as were the table, altar, and ark. Nothing suits God's presence but the best and purest. The value of the material increases as we approach from the court to the shrine. Beyond the veil was the holy Oracle, God's side: the holy place was the people's side. The gorgeous hanging, with its magnificent colors of blue, purple, and scarlet, parted the one room from the other, thus "signifying, that the way into the holiest of all was not yet made manifest," for redemption was only pledged, not yet an actual fact. Jesus must die before access to God for all men who will draw near could be secured.

1. *The Candlestick.*
(Ex. 25: 31-39; 37: 17-24.)

(1) The candlestick had a central shaft from which six arms or branches, three on each side, and each surmounted by a lamp, curved upward to a level with the lamp on the shaft. So it is represented on the bas-relief on the Arch of Titus at Rome. "It was a peculiarity of the candlestick that all the branches were on the same plane." A talent of gold ($27,375) was used in its construction. The lamps were lighted every evening at sunset and burnt till morning, when the high priest "dressed" them (Ex. 30: 7, 8). A statute obligated the children of Israel to furnish "oil beaten for the light, to cause a lamp to burn continually" (Ex. 27: 20, R. V.; Lev. 24: 2). It

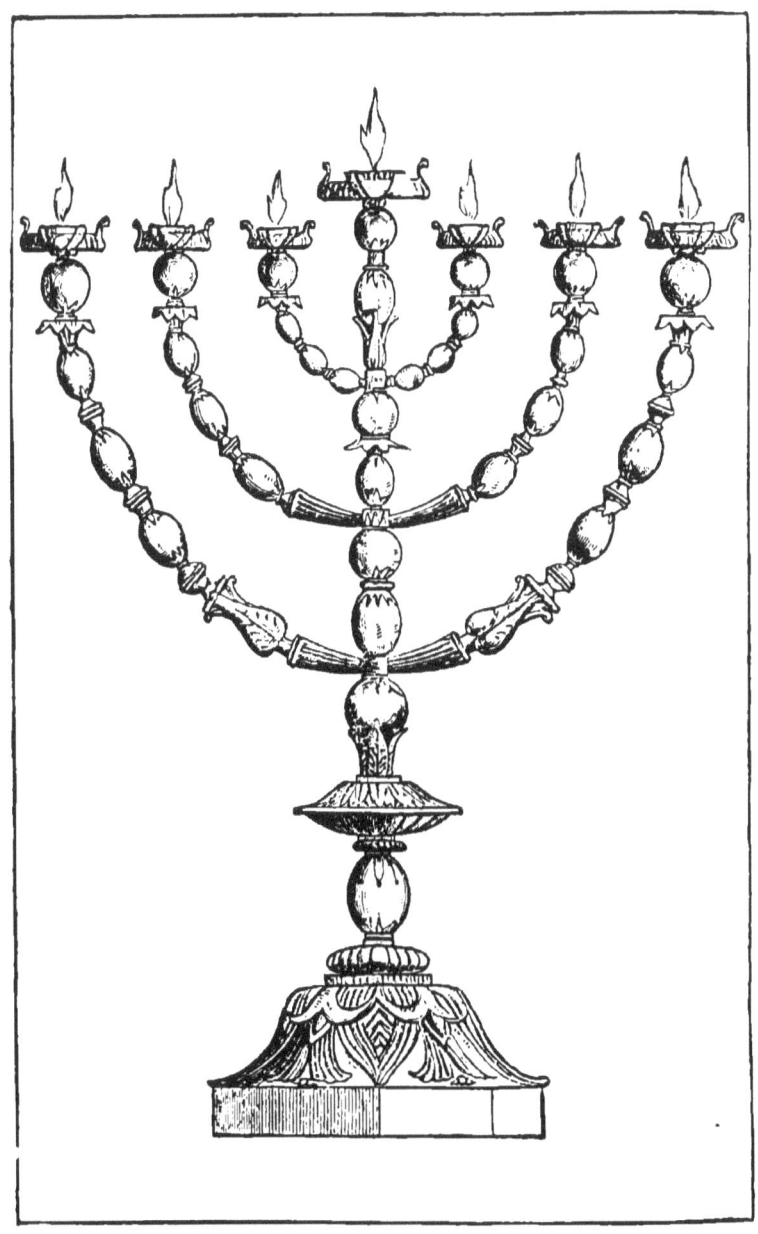

FROM MODEL. THE GOLDEN CANDLESTICK.

was placed on the south side of the room (Ex. 40 : 24), and shed its light directly on the table, which stood opposite, on the north side, and on the altar of incense, which was set in the center and near the veil. The design of the candlestick was to furnish light for the holy place, and thus enable the priests to perform the prescribed ministry therein.

(2) The *typical meaning* of the candlestick does not depend on our reasoning nor on logical deductions. Happily, the Bible itself furnishes us with the needed information. Light is one of the commonest biblical figures of speech. It is used to designate the holiness and immaculate purity of God, who is "light, and in him is no darkness at all" (I. John 1 : 5); Christ, who is "the light of the world" (John 8 : 12); and Christians, who to those who are in spiritual darkness are also "the light of the world" (Matt. 5 : 14). It is to Christ and believers more particularly that the great chandelier in the tabernacle was intended to witness. And there are two passages of scripture which perhaps more than any others illustrate and expound its significant teaching. These two passages are Revelation 1 : 10-20 and Zechariah 4. They teach a twofold lesson : First, the church is designed to be a faithful witness for the Lord, and to shine for

him amid the world's gloom. Second, the church's shining power depends solely on the grace and Spirit of the Lord Jesus Christ.

Revelation 1 : 10-20 records a most imposing vision, the glorified Redeemer in the midst of his church. It was seen by John on the Lord's day, that is, certainly, the first day of the week, the Christian Sabbath. "The Lord's day" and "the day of the Lord" are never used in the New Testament interchangeably, or as convertible terms. (Cf. I. Cor. 11 : 20 —"the Lord's supper," and Rev. 19 : 17 —"the supper of the great God.")

The whole church of Christ of John's time and of all time is represented by seven golden candlesticks (Rev. 1 : 11, 12, 20). Seven is the sacred number, the number of completeness and perfection. Gold, too, is the sacred metal, the metal of the sanctuary.

In the midst of the candlesticks walked the Son of God (vs. 13-17). His dress indicates his priestly dignity and regal authority. He is the Defender, Provider, and Judge of the church. Its relation to him is that of dependence, loyalty, and witness-bearing. Its life and its light are communicated by him. Without him neither is possible. In the vision Christ is seen, like Aaron of old, *dressing* the lamps, correcting, instructing, warning the churches as they severally need.

Obviously, the symbolism is drawn bodily from the great candlestick of the tent and the temple, and from the priestly functions connected therewith. It is New Testament truth in the dress of Old Testament symbol that we are here shown, and the two match exactly. The one sole business of the candlestick was to give light. For this end it was made, furnished with lamps and oil, and was dressed and cared for by the attendant priest. Apart from this it had no right to exist. The one prime object of the church is, likewise, to shed light, to shine, that the glory of Christ, who has redeemed it with his precious blood, may be manifested, and that they who sit in darkness may have light. Its business is to be a lightholder, a lampstand (Phil. 2 : 15, 16). "For God, who commanded the light to shine out of darkness, hath shined in our hearts, to give the light of the knowledge of the glory of God in the face of Jesus Christ" (II. Cor. 4 : 6). He shined *in*, that they might shine *out*. For this end the church is called and chosen. For this end Christ endows and enriches it with his Spirit, gifts, and graces; rules, supplies, and dresses it. If it fail or refuse to shine, it becomes both useless and hurtful, a cumberer and hindrance. Better no street lamp-post on a dark night than one unlit or gone out; the danger is less for the belated passer. Better no professing body than one that has quenched its light—that has lost its illuminating power.

Zechariah 4 contains a vision which presents another and very important feature of the general truth taught by the great light of the tabernacle. The details of the vision are simple and clear. No more description of it is required than will put us in possession of the main facts. The candlestick had a bowl upon the top of it, and seven lamps, and seven pipes which connected the lamps with the bowl. (The Revision reads, "seven pipes to each of the lamps.") Two olive trees, one on each side of the bowl, furnished the oil needed for the light.

The central principle of the vision is verse 6: "Not by might, nor by power, but by my Spirit, saith the Lord of hosts." This vital truth is illustrated by the relation of the lamps to the bowl, and of the bowl to the olive trees. The two sons of oil (see margin) supplied the bowl; the bowl supplied the lamps. Without the trees the bowl was altogether useless; without the flow of the oil to the lamps the candlestick was likewise useless. The application of the vision to God's people in the prophet's time, and to us of the present day, is not difficult.

(*a*) The power to shine lies in the oil, and in

the oil alone. It need not be repeated that oil is the scriptural symbol for the gift and grace of the Spirit. The Lord by his Spirit is the only power that can make a believer's life bright and fruitful. Apart from him we can do nothing (John 15:5). The wick in the lamp is for one single purpose, to convey the oil from the bowl to the flame. Even faith, precious as it is, has no more virtue in itself than the wick. Faith is the conductor of grace, not its source. No Christian is a fountain of light or of power in himself. "Our sufficiency is of God" (II. Cor. 3:5). We know what the result is when a lamp is lit which contains no oil: all it can do is to smolder and smoke, and give forth an offensive odor. We know just as well how dark and cheerless our life is, how false and hollow the *pretensions* to shining, when the flow of grace is obstructed or arrested.

(*b*) The supply is inexhaustible (II. Cor. 9:8). The seven lamps could not, by any possibility, exhaust the fullness of the bowl, for it was constantly fed and filled by the olive trees. No more can the whole church exhaust the grace of God in Christ (Phil. 4:19). It matters not how many draw, or how often, or how much: the supply is ample for all. Grace abounds, grace *reigns*. The water in the reservoir of a great city never runs low, for it is always filling. No matter how great the drain on the reservoir, there is no diminution. As a watchman of such a one once said when asked about the danger of running short, "it makes no odds up here."[1]

(c) Note, also, that the flow is without effort or toil. It was the business of the two sons of oil to furnish all that was required. The bowl, pipes, lamps, wicks, had nothing to do either to create or to increase the quantity needed. The supply was not dependent on human inventions. The trees, without man's devices, and without his help, furnished all and furnished abundance. It is "not by might, nor by power, but by my Spirit." It is the Lord's work to supply, ours to receive. As much as we need, and up to the full measure of our need, we may draw; we can neither lower the supply, nor take more than we can use. Just what the lamp can consume will the wick draw, and no more; it cannot hoard. Nor can we. A present supply for present need is the ruling principle.

2. *The Table of Showbread.*
(Ex. 25 : 23-30; Lev. 24 : 5-9.)

The table of showbread was set on the north side of the holy place and directly opposite the candlestick. It was made with a "border" and a "crown," terms which, according to Soltau and

[1] Brooke.

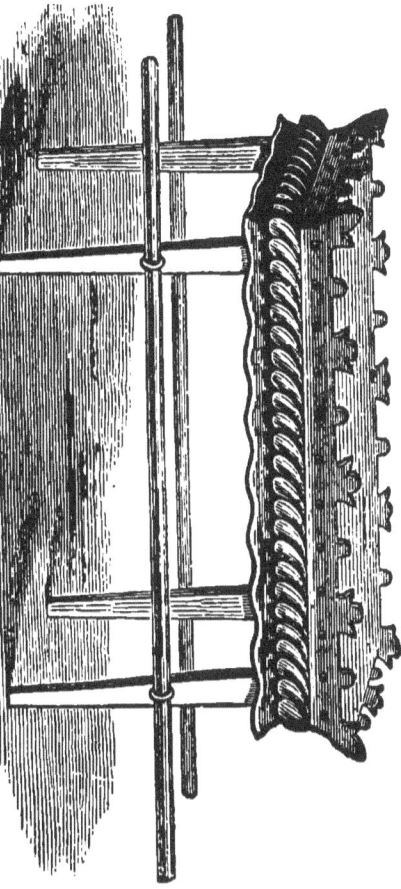

TABLE OF SHOWBREAD. Scale—1 inch to cubit. From Model.

Newton, designate two different things; namely, the border being the elevated edges running round the table, and the crown being another elevation within the plane of the table. The first was intended to secure the golden vessels (Ex. 25 : 29) connected with it, and the other the twelve loaves.

The name, "table of showbread," is derived not so much from the table itself as from the bread placed on it. It was the Bread of Presence or Presentation (lit., "bread of the face") that is meant (Matt. 12 : 4). Its design was not an acknowledgment by the people of their dependence on God for their food, nor of their gratitude for their temporal supplies, though these ideas may be remotely suggested by it; but it was a memorial before God continually (Lev. 24 : 7). In this verse it is expressly said that the frankincense which was spread over the loaves was "for a memorial." On the removal of the stale bread and the supply of fresh (which occurred every Sabbath), the frankincense was burned on the golden altar (so much is inferred from Lev. 24 : 7, 8). The vessels of the table must have been used for this purpose, for none are here mentioned as belonging to the altar.[1] This ceremony con-

---

[1] The Revision gives Numbers 4: 12 thus: "And they shall take all the vessels of ministry, wherewith they minister in the sanctuary, and put them in a cloth of blue," etc. This neither affirms nor denies that the altar of incense had vessels of its own.

nected the table and altar, and it shows, moreover, that the bread and the incense belonged peculiarly to God, and were not merely an expression of the gratitude of the people for their material supplies. The bread of presence was a perpetual memorial unto God of his chosen people. There were twelve loaves, one for each tribe. All were represented—little Benjamin as well as royal Judah, and Dan as certainly as the priestly Levi. And there was just as much for the one tribe as for another. No part of God's family was overlooked or forgotten; each was as fully presented as it could be. And they were always before him (Ex. 25: 30). Never for a moment were they out of his sight—the continuous reminder to him, as we may say, of his covenant relation to them, of his promises and mighty pledges to be their God and Redeemer.

Nor are they forgotten amid their national dismemberment and dispersion and the sorrows of their exile. Their Memorial has not perished. Jesus of Nazareth, a Jew according to the flesh, who died for that nation in a sense in which he died for no other (John 11: 51, 52), is now their Bread of Remembrance before the face of God continually. "And now I stand and am judged for the hope of the promise made of God unto our fathers: unto which promise our twelve tribes, instantly serving God day and night, hope to come," are Paul's noble words to King Agrippa. "Our twelve tribes hope to come"! Unbelief may stupidly stare about and ask, Where are the twelve tribes? Our answer is: Their Memorial is on high, and in God's good time they will be restored: Jerusalem shall yet be the joy of the whole earth, the center of blessing for the world (cf. Rom. 11).

Furthermore, what the bread of presence was for Israel in the olden time, Jesus Christ now is for all his people. He is all that the loaves symbolized. He is before God in his public character. The Father sees in him not only his well-beloved Son, but likewise the Representative and Surety of the saved from among men. They are in him, and as being united with him they, too, are before the Father. All Israel was before the face of God in the twelve loaves. All believers are in his presence in the person of the Saviour. "For we being many are one bread, and one body" (I. Cor. 10: 17). Christ in the glory is at once the pledge and the assurance that the inheritance is safe for believers, and they are safe for it (I. Pet. 1: 3-5): "For all the promises of God in him are yea, and in him Amen, unto the glory of God by us" (II. Cor. 1: 20). Every believer is there in him—the most obscure and humble equally with the most illustrious, the weakest as well as the strongest; not one is ignored, nor one forgotten.

Again, the bread, when removed from the table, was eaten by the priests in the holy place (Lev. 24: 9). The antitype is found in our communion with the Father through the Son. But before the bread was eaten the frankincense was carefully gathered and burned as an offering to the Lord, probably on the altar of incense. Here, then, is the union of the table and the altar; that is, communion is grounded in intercession. We have fellowship with the Father through the Son, who is now in his presence for us. Besides, it must not be forgotten that the priests are always the type of the people of God, while the high priest is that of Christ. Accordingly, we have in this rich symbol of the table the Lord Jesus as the True Bread for the sustenance of the family of God. He is God's infinite provision for our hungry souls. How appropriate, satisfying, and enriching he is, need not now be told, for all who have tasted see and know that the Lord is *good*. "Eat, O friends; drink, yea, drink abundantly, O beloved" (S. of S. 5: 1).

3. *The Golden Altar of Incense.*
(Ex. 30: 1-10.)

(1) *The place of this altar in the description of the tabernacle and its furniture is peculiar.* Its

THE GOLDEN ALTAR.

"natural place," writes Rawlinson in the "Pulpit Commentary" on Exodus, "would seem to have been chapter 25: 10-40"; and he goes so far as to say that whether it was an omission from that chapter which Moses afterward supplied, or whether Divine wisdom saw fit to give the directions in the order we now have them, "cannot be determined." This is unworthy of so great and good a student of the Bible. Whether or not we are able to explain the difficulties of the Bible, our duty as loyal believers in God's Word is reverently to receive it. There is, however, an explanation for the seeming irregularity in the description of the tabernacle furniture which is quite satisfactory to the present writer at least. Exodus 25-27 describes the tabernacle and its contents, the altar of sacrifice, and the court. In chapters 28 and 29 we have the record of the appointment of Aaron and his sons, the description of the high priest's vestments, and the directions for their consecration. But in all these chapters there is not a word about the altar of incense or the laver. Chapter 30 appoints these, orders the ransom money, the making of the holy oil and the holy incense. In chapters 25-27 the mercy-seat and the brazen altar are brought together, thus symbolizing the fundamental truth that acceptance with God is founded upon atonement. In chapter 30 the altar of incense and the laver are brought together, because communion and purification are inseparably connected. There can be no communion where defilement is present. Between the ark and the brazen altar on the one hand and the golden altar and the laver on the other, stands the priesthood, indispensable to both. Reconciliation with God is first, and precedes every other relation of the sinner with God, in the divine order; sanctification and fellowship follow it; and both are indissolubly bound up with the divinely appointed priesthood.

Furthermore, the expression, "And the Lord spake unto Moses, saying," is of very frequent occurrence in the middle books of the Pentateuch. In every instance where it is introduced it marks a fresh revelation from Jehovah, and hence a new division. The Revisers of the Old Testament recognize this fact, and begin a paragraph with each repetition of the phrase. Particularly is it noticeable in Exodus 30.

Now it is very significant that in Exodus 25:1 the phrase in question is found, and not again until 30:11; that is, between Exodus 25:1 and 30:11 it is omitted. Accordingly, the whole section lying between these two verses forms a continuous revelation, and is a unit. It begins with the ark (25:10), and ends with the altar of incense (30 : 1-10). "That which is first in design is last in execution, is a law which even philosophy delights to enforce and illustrate."[1] The main design of the tabernacle and its rites was *worship*, communion with the living God, the God of Israel, who dwelt among the chosen people. This it was the preëminent aim of the incense-altar to set forth. The golden altar is the climax of all, the goal of the revelation contained in Exodus 25–30: 10. Hence it is the last prescribed.

In Exodus 30: 11-38 four times the phrase, "And the Lord spake unto Moses," is found. The subject of these verses is, The Conditions of Acceptable Worship. Four things are indispensable to it: (*a*) redemption (vs. 12-16); (*b*) purification (vs. 17-21); (*c*) anointing (vs. 22-33), that is, the presence of the Spirit; (*d*) pure incense (vs. 34-38)—adoration, supplication, intercession. There is such a thing in the Bible as *structural inspiration*. The arrangement of the divine communications in Exodus 25–30 is evidence of it.

(2) *The Position of the Golden Altar.* It stood before the veil, and directly in front of the mercy-seat in the most holy place (Ex. 30: 6; 40: 5). Although the veil interposed between it and the ark, nevertheless God speaks of it as before the

[1] Erdman.

ark, as if nothing intervened,—"the altar which is before the Lord" (Lev. 4: 18). It sustained, therefore, most intimate relations with the ark and the mercy-seat, and with the presence of God, the Shechinah (Heb. 9: 4).[1]

(3) *The Incense Burned Upon the Altar* (Ex. 30: 34-38). Just what were the ingredients of which the incense was compounded, cannot be satisfactorily determined. Much that is written about it is mere conjecture. It is pretty generally agreed that the expression "tempered together" (v. 35) should be "salted" (cf. Lev. 2: 13). It is described as "pure and holy," and "most holy." The people were strictly forbidden to make any incense or perfume like it. It was for God alone. Morning and evening the high priest, Aaron, was to burn the incense on the altar.

(4) *The altar of incense was closely connected with the altar of sacrifice.* The coals of fire by

[1] By the expression "golden censer" of Hebrews 9:4 is most probably meant the altar of incense. Exodus 30: 6; 40: 5, closely connect the golden altar with the ark and mercy-seat. The language of I. Kings 6: 22 seems decisive: "Also the whole altar that was by the oracle"—"that belonged to the oracle" (R.V.). We know that the golden altar was placed near the ark and was separated from it only by the veil; and by its position and the priestly functions performed at it, it seems to have been regarded as belonging rather to the holy of holies than to the holy place. Besides, if there was a golden censer kept in the most holy place and employed only on the Day of Atonement, how was it brought from thence? The high priest's first entrance was with a censer full of coals of fire and incense (Lev. 16: 12). That censer could not have been kept in the most holy place, for it would have been inaccessible to the priest. (For a convincing exegesis of the passage, see Delitzsch on Hebrews.)

which the incense was burned were taken from the altar in the court (Lev. 16: 12; cf. 10: 1). The blood of the sin-offering, which was slain at the brazen altar, was also sprinkled on the horns of the golden altar, thus bringing the two into very close relation.

(5) *The altar of incense symbolized communion with God in prayer and worship* (Ex. 30: 36). "Let my prayer be set forth before thee as incense, and the lifting up of my hands as the evening sacrifice" (Ps. 141: 2). In Revelation 5: 8 we read of the vials or bowls of incense "which are the prayers of saints." Note: (*a*) The altar was "before the Lord," was intimately related to the throne of God. Prayer brings us into the presence of the Searcher of hearts. (*b*) Acceptable prayer rests on the atoning work of Christ. The blood of the sacrifice for sin was put upon its horns. The appeal of the suppliant was backed by the appeal of the blood of expiation which was lifted up by the four horns. No prayer or cry to God can avail that does not rest on the blood of Christ. (*c*) Acceptable prayer must be accompanied with purification. The priests washed their hands and feet at the laver before entering the holy place. Those parts of their person which came into constant contact with defilement needed constant cleansing. "I will

therefore that men pray every where, lifting up holy hands, without wrath and doubting" (I. Tim. 2 : 8). (*d*) Prayer is a daily duty (Ex. 30 : 7, 8). "Perpetual incense before the Lord" reminds us of the apostolic injunction, "Pray without ceasing" (I. Thes. 5 : 17).

(6) *It symbolized prayer in conjunction with Christ's intercession.* In Revelation 8 : 3, 4, we read that much incense was offered at the golden altar with the prayers of all the saints. The reference is unmistakably to the altar of incense and its design. It is not needful to identify this angel with Christ, though he is represented under this name in the book. The angel who, with uplifted hand, makes his most solemn asseveration in chapter 10, is Christ (cf. Dan. 12 : 7). The two sickle visions (Rev. 14 : 14-20) relate to the time of the end, when Christ will first gather his own wheat to himself, and next the wicked for their doom (cf. Matt. 13 : 40-43). Angels will be the executors of his will, but he himself is present and orders all. Observe, the passage clearly distinguishes between the incense and the prayers. The incense is added to the prayers, mingles with the prayers, perfumes them, and makes them acceptable to God. The teaching is, that Christ's intercession purifies, perfects, and renders acceptable to God the supplications of the saints. With-

out his presence and merit no prayer, however urgent and fervent, would ever reach the divine ear.

(7) *It symbolized the efficacy of His intercession.* Each ingredient composing the holy incense was of equal weight with the others (Ex. 30 : 34), and all of them were salted together and most holy. The symbol presents the idea of the equality and uniformity of the work and perfections of the Lord Jesus. In him no one feature, or grace, or attribute preponderates over another. In him all is adjusted with infinite precision. Justice does not override mercy; pity does not displace truth; righteousness does not overbalance love. All is right and holy and good. Therefore, our Advocate is a perfect and a prevailing One. Moreover, we must remember the close relation of the two altars. The blood shed at the one was put on the horns of the other. In the brazen altar we have Christ in the value of his atoning sacrifice; in the golden altar we have him in the value of his intercession. But the latter is bound up with the former. Because of his perfect work for us on the cross, we know how perfect and efficacious is his work for us now in glory (Rom. 8 : 34; Heb. 9 : 25).

4. *The Veil.*
(Ex. 26 : 31-33; Heb. 10 : 19-22.)

The veil to which reference is made is that which separated between the holy and most holy place, called in Hebrews 9:3 "the second veil." It was made of fine twined linen, in blue, purple, and scarlet, interwoven with cherubic figures. The wise-hearted women furnished it (Ex. 35:25). In Hebrews 10:19, 20, we are told that we have "liberty" or "boldness to enter into the holiest by the blood of Jesus, by a new and living way, which he hath consecrated for us, through the veil, that is to say, his flesh." Here is inspired authority for teaching the typical significance of the rending of the temple veil at the death of Christ. In all its outward form and circumstance a more humiliating and shameful death than that of being crucified as one with two convicted felons our Lord could not have suffered. On the one side of that dreadful cross was God with averted face; on the other, Satan exulting in his triumph. The world took sides with Satan. "His darling was in the power of the dog," and there was none to pity, none to help. Wicked men and the devil sought one day of free action, unrestrained liberty, and they employed it in crucifying the Son of God. But here, as in so many other instances, Samson's riddle becomes God's riddle — "Out of the eater came forth meat, and out of the strong came forth sweetness" (Judg. 14:14). By his cross Jesus spoiled principalities and powers, making an open show of them. By

THE ARK OF THE COVENANT.

it the way was laid bare for all who will to enter into the holiest, for "the veil of the temple was rent in twain from the top to the bottom" (Mark 15: 38). That veil was no old, thin, faded piece of drapery, but a new and strong fabric. Jewish authority attests that it was four inches in thickness, tightly woven, and renewed each year. No human power rent it. Two unseen hands of superhuman strength grasped the firm hanging at the top and tore it downward to the very bottom, and flung it apart, so that the mercy-seat was made visible, and the way to the awful Presence unobstructed.

Jesus' death was voluntary. Neither man nor devil took his life from him. He laid it down of himself (John 10:18). He gave himself for us. Matthew's expressive words are, "Jesus ... yielded up his spirit" (Matt. 27:50, R. V.). Access to God is now made manifest, for an infinite expiation has been presented. We may draw near with boldness, with a true heart, in full assurance of faith, for the new and living way hath been consecrated for us by the blood of Jesus '(Heb. 10:19-22).

5. *The Ark of the Covenant.*
(Ex. 25:10-22.)

The ark of the covenant was the only object found in the holy of holies, and it was the most sacred object of the tabernacle. About it the most important of the Mosaic rites arranged themselves. It was the center of the whole symbolic service. Every act of worship was related directly or indirectly to the ark. It was a chest or coffer of acacia wood, covered with a heavy plating of gold within and without. It was two and a half cubits in length, and a cubit and a half in depth and breadth. Its lid, or covering, was a slab of pure gold, held firmly in its place by the crown of gold (the elevated edges of the ark) into which it was closely fitted. This covering was the Mercy-seat. From its ends rose the Cherubim, which were formed out of the gold of the mercy-seat itself, not separate attachments. Their wings were projected over their heads and forward, thus forming a sort of canopy for the ark. Their faces were turned toward each other, their eyes bent downward toward the mercy-seat.

(1) *The Cherubim.* Of these symbolic figures no exhaustive study can be here attempted, yet some general observations touching them seem to be in place. They are first mentioned in Genesis 3: 24, where they are represented as the guardians of the Garden of Eden and of the tree of life. Here they make their appearance immediately after the fall. Next, they are found in the veil, curtains, and ark of the tabernacle. In Ezekiel

1 : 5-26 a marvelous description is given of them, one that associates them most intimately with the throne of God, and one which seems to preclude the opinion, held by many, that they symbolize redeemed humanity. Revelation 4, 5, reveals to us four living creatures (or beings) that almost certainly must be identified with the cherubim of other scripture. Here likewise they belong to the throne. If we are to follow the revised text of this book, these four living creatures must be distinguished from the redeemed: "For thou wast slain, and didst purchase unto God with thy blood *men* of every tribe, and tongue, and people, and nation, and madest *them* to be unto our God a kingdom and priests," etc. (Rev. 5 : 9, 10, R. V.). The attitude of the cherubim, gazing on the mercy-seat, reminds one of the words of Peter, who represents the angels as desiring to look intently into the mystery of redemption (I. Pet. 1: 12). But they seem not to be designed to prefigure the angels. Less still are they to be taken as symbols of the four Gospels, or as the heads of redeemed creation. Two things are very manifest with respect to them: First, they are intimately associated with the throne of God. Both Ezekiel and John in the Apocalypse make this clear. Even in the ark they are connected with the throne, for such the ark was. Second,

they are closely connected with the judicial government of the Most High, and appear to be executors of the divine will. With the speed of the lightning-flash they come and go, doing the behests of Him who is on the throne above them, according to Ezekiel. In the Revelation they are connected with the providential judgments which are inflicted on the wicked.

The view that commends itself as being more satisfactory than perhaps any other, is that which regards the cherubim as *hieroglyphs* of certain divine attributes, as justice, righteousness, truth, and mercy. They, together with the sword, guard the way of the tree of life; and yet the sword one day awakes against the man who is Jehovah's fellow (Zech. 13:7). Mercy toward the lost and justice on behalf of the Throne unite and embrace in the cross of Christ. Over the mercy-seat the cherubim stand, guarding and overshadowing, yet with fixed gaze they behold the blood of atonement sprinkled there, which satisfies every claim of law and justice, and harmonizes all the attributes of God. By virtue of the shed blood justice and righteousness can unite with mercy and love in the pardon and acceptance of the guilty.

(2) *The Contents of the Ark*. First of all, within it was the Testimony, that is, the two tables of stone engraved by the finger of God (Ex. 25:21;

40 : 20). Next, the Pot of Manna (Heb. 9 : 4; Ex. 16 : 33). The manna was laid up in the ark "before the testimony," that is, in front of the two tables. The "hidden manna" of Revelation 2 : 17 is an allusion to the pot of manna in the ark. Finally, it contained Aaron's Rod that budded (Num. 17: 10; Heb. 9 : 4). It appears from the account in Numbers that the rod was kept for a time in the tabernacle, as a witness against the rebels, before it was deposited in the ark. The sacred chest, however, was designed chiefly to be the depository for the tables of the covenant, the Decalogue. These two tables lay at the base of all the other laws of Moses, and constituted the very essence of the covenant relation of Israel with God.

(3) *The ark was God's throne*, the place where he met with the priest, and communicated his will for the instruction and guidance of his people (Ex. 25 : 22; Ps. 80 : 1). Its form resembles a throne, of which the mercy-seat was the base, the cherubim the sides and supports, and their wings the canopy. It can hardly be doubted that it is the foundation for the beautiful and significant expression, "the throne of grace" (Heb. 4 : 16). For it was here that expiation for sins was effected, here that reconciliation between the holy Lord and his offending people was wrought, and

here that mercy and forgiveness were bestowed on the guilty. As the ark was the place where the divine manifestation took place, and pardon and blessing were dispensed by Him who dwelt there, it is called "the throne of judgment," "the throne of righteousness."

(4) *The Mercy-Seat.* It is not too much to say that this was the supreme feature of the tabernacle, and of the Mosaic rites. It is spoken of in the Scriptures not simply as the lid or covering of the ark, but as a distinct object, almost as if it did not belong to the ark (Ex. 30:6; 31:7; 35:12, etc.). In Leviticus 16:2 we have "the mercy-seat, which is upon the ark." In Numbers 7:89, R.V., we read, "And when Moses went into the tent of meeting to speak with him, then he heard the Voice speaking unto him from above the mercy-seat that was upon the ark of the testimony, from between the two cherubim." These passages remove the mercy-seat from anything like a secondary or subordinate place, a mere appendage of the ark, and invest it with the utmost importance. In I. Chronicles 28:11 the holy of holies is called "the place [R. V. marg., "house"] of the mercy-seat" (*beth-hakkap-poreth*). Both the Septuagint and the Vulgate render this phrase "the house of propitiation." The reason for the application of this name to it is discovered in the intimate

relation which subsists between the mercy-seat and the atonement for sins which was effected thereat. The blood of the sin-offering was sprinkled on it, whereby propitiation was made (Lev. 16 : 13, 14, 16). For this reason the mercy-seat is called "the propitiatory" ($ἰλαστήριον$) in Hebrews 9 : 5; because it was the place where the atonement was completed, where satisfaction to the divine claims was made, and where pacification was secured by the covering (atonement) of the sins of the people. Beneath it were the two tables, the Ten Words, which testified: first, that God's government is founded on justice and righteousness; second, that Israel was in covenant relation with him; third, that their sins were ever present before him, and that he was perfectly acquainted with their rebellious ways (Deut. 31 : 26, 27). The blood on the mercy-seat met the demands of the law and satisfied the claims of justice, for it covered the sins from the Divine presence, obliterating them altogether. The attitude of the cherubim attests the complete pardon and acceptance of the guilty people. For if they are the symbols of certain attributes we can readily perceive how, with their eyes fixed on the Propitiatory, they seem to declare that mercy and truth are here met together, righteousness and peace kiss each other (Ps. 85 : 10, 11).

What the mercy-seat did ceremonially or symbolically for Israel, Christ accomplishes perfectly and graciously for all believers, for him "God hath set forth to be a propitiation through faith in his blood" (Rom. 3: 25). God hath presented, put forward, his own Son as a mercy-seat, and so he is now justified in justifying the ungodly, even, who believe in Jesus. The throne of judgment is now the throne of grace to which we may confidently and confidingly come.

Nor is this all. The ark sometimes served as a leader and guide to the people, particularly when difficulties arose or dangers threatened. It went before the congregation a three days' journey once (Num. 10: 33). God proved to his people that he, not Hobab, would be to them "instead of eyes." It went before them at the passage of the Jordan, and at the capture of Jericho. Nor has God forgotten his pledge that is bound up in the very name—*ark of the covenant;* for in one of the apocalyptic visions it is seen in the opened temple, the enduring witness of his faithfulness to Israel (Rev. 11: 19).

VII. TYPICAL SIGNIFICANCE OF THE TABERNACLE.

We may dismiss as unworthy of consideration the Jewish absurdities of its being the symbol of the heavens, and German vagaries of its being a type of man in his complex constitution of body, soul, and spirit. Let us rather seek the true import of this ancient structure from the Word of God.

1. *It symbolized God's presence with his chosen people.* When the command was given to Moses to build a sanctuary, the Lord said, "Let them make me a sanctuary; that I may dwell among them" (Ex. 25: 8). "And I will dwell among the children of Israel, and will be their God" (Ex. 29: 45). This, then, was one main purpose of the tabernacle, this its chief aim,—to represent the sublime truth which is so often insisted on in other scripture, namely, that God actually does so draw near his people as that it may be truthfully said that he dwells with them, and makes his home among them. The language of the New Testament is just as explicit. In II. Corinthians 6: 16 the Spirit of God thus testifies: "For ye are the temple of the living God; as God hath said, I will dwell in them, and walk in them; and I will be their God, and they shall be my people."

2. *Another design of the tabernacle was to show how completely God identified himself with his chosen flock.* He dwelt among them, making a tent his abode, himself a Pilgrim and Wayfarer as they. If there were obstructions to be encountered, if hardships were to be borne, if enemies to be

met, he would share in every trouble and every danger. "In all their afflictions he was afflicted." His identity with them was so close that assaults against them he resented as aimed against himself, as we see in the instances of Amalek and Balaam. He might have serious dealings with his people on account of their follies and sins, as we know he often had. But this was discipline in his own family—the authority he wielded and the obedience he required in his own house. But these were matters to be adjusted between himself and those whom he had brought into covenant relation with him. He would not permit a stranger to intermeddle therewith.

It was in virtue of God's presence in the tabernacle that holiness was so repeatedly enjoined upon Israel (Lev. 20: 26; 21: 8, etc.), and all impurity and uncleanness so strictly forbidden (Num. 5: 3, etc.). It was his dwelling among them that made them all they were, and what they were—a peculiar people, a separate and holy people, God's own possession and portion. All this was a historical reality in Israel. Nevertheless, it was a type, an adumbration, of something better and more glorious—for the church now, and for the redeemed in glory. God now identifies himself with his children even in a more intimate way than in the tabernacle (John 14: 23; Eph.

2 : 20-22; I. John 4 : 16). He once dwelt *among* his people; now he dwells *in* them.

But this type looks forward to a still more majestic realization. It will find its last and most complete fulfillment when the eternal City of God shall descend out of heaven and glorify the redeemed earth with its effulgent light, its unapproachable splendor; when it shall at length be proclaimed, "The tabernacle of God is with men, and he will dwell with them, and they shall be his people, and God himself shall be with them, and be their God" (Rev. 21 : 3).

3. *It was a remarkable illustration of God's method of bringing sinners to himself.* "Having therefore, brethren, boldness to enter into the holiest by the blood of Jesus, by a new and living way, which he hath consecrated for us, through the veil, that is to say, his flesh; and having an High Priest over the house of God; let us draw near with a true heart, in full assurance of faith" (Heb. 10 : 19-22). Three great truths are embraced in this passage : First, an accepted sacrifice, by which the sins of all believers are expiated and put away. Second, an opened sanctuary. Christians are now admitted into the very presence of God, and stand before him accepted in the same measure as the blessed Redeemer himself. Third, a glorious Intercessor, whose

plea for his people never fails, because based on his own finished work. But now it must be apparent to all readers of the Epistle to the Hebrews, that the inspired writer is here, as in so many other places, drawing his imagery from the rites observed at the tabernacle, and clothing his thoughts in the priestly and sacrificial language of the sanctuary of the wilderness. Just as an Israelite could approach God only by means of blood, so Christians now come to God through the blood of Christ, who is both the Sacrifice and the Priest. Access to God beyond the veil in the olden time was only through the blood of atonement. Access to God now in heaven is not otherwise. It is, it can only be, by means of the Great High Priest who offered himself without spot unto God. For a thousand years and more God taught his people by a mighty object-lesson that salvation comes alone through propitiation for sins. The tabernacle was a parable and a picture, graphic and vivid, of God's way of saving the lost.

The same vital truth is taught in Hebrews 9 : 23 : "It was therefore necessary that the patterns [copies] of things in the heavens should be purified with these; but the heavenly things themselves with better sacrifices than these." This verse is not without considerable difficulty. In what sense are we to understand the tabernacle and its services to be copies of things in the heavens? Certainly the earthly sanctuary was not a literal diagram of the unseen world. The universe is not built after the fashion of the tent, with its two compartments and its court. What the verse seems to teach is this: that there is a correspondence between the way to the mercy-seat in the tabernacle and the way to God's presence on high. That way is by blood. The one is the "copy" of the other. There is no access to God but through atonement. What is meant by "the heavenly things themselves," which must be purified by better sacrifices, that is, by Christ's sacrifice? The answer seems to be, *heaven*. Verse 24 makes this plain; Jesus has entered into heaven itself now to appear in the presence of God for us. But how did God's uncreated abode require purification? Surely not as being defiled by sin. Scripture represents it as the place of untroubled light and blessedness. The answer is not to be sought by substituting some other word for "purify," as *consecrate*. The term to be supplied in the last clause of the verse must surely be that found in the first clause, namely, "purify." The thought appears to us to be this: God's forgiving mercy and saving grace could reach the lost only through an adequate atonement. His justice and law must be vindicated, his wrath appeased, and every charge against the guilty be canceled in righteousness, before he could pardon and save. This was the supreme necessity. And Christ did meet fully and forever the tremendous necessity. By his own blood he entered into the holy place and settled the question of sin for believers before the face of God (vs. 11-14). Our Great Priest satisfied God perfectly about sin, and obtained eternal redemption for us. By him we now come to God, and have the right and privilege to come. By him we have the same measure of acceptance with the Father, and the same standing, as Jesus himself. The new and living way to God is now opened to all who will draw near.

4. *It was a prophecy of Christ's incarnation.* In John 1 : 14 occurs this weighty sentence: "And the Word was made flesh [became flesh], and dwelt among us, (and we beheld his glory, the glory as of the only begotten of the Father,) full of grace and truth." The incarnation is here asserted. The Son of God assumed human nature —took unto himself a "true body and reasonable soul." He did not cease to be the Word, the Son of God, when he became man. For John immediately adds that he dwelt among us—he, the eternal Word. Literally, it is, "He tabernacled with us." The use of this picturesque term points

to the tabernacle and the presence of the Lord in its most holy place. This is put beyond a doubt by the words following—"and we beheld [contemplated] his glory, the glory as of the only begotten of the Father."[1] When the tabernacle was completed and set up according to the divine directions, we are told that the glory of the Lord filled it (Ex. 40:34). Thus John connects the incarnation and personal presence of the Son among men with the earlier presence of the Lord with his people in the wilderness. He there dwelt with them, and walked among them (Lev. 26:11, 12; II. Sam. 7:6). But now he is come to take up his permanent abode with men by "wedding himself forever to their flesh." This word "tabernacled" (ἐσκήνωσεν) is peculiar to John, and is employed to denote a permanent stay, an everlasting abode (Rev. 7:15; 12:12; 13:6; 21:3). Besides, it should be remembered that Jesus identified his own body with the "temple" (John 2:19). Thus the building of a house for the Lord, and his visible occupancy of it, was a pre-

---

[1] The term "glory" (δοξα) carries on the parallel between the tabernacle and the incarnation already indicated by the phrase, "tabernacled among us." As the Shechinah dwelt in the most holy place (Ex. 40:34; I. Kings 8:11), so the divine glory dwelt in the person of Christ, even during his humiliation. The dazzling brightness with which his person glowed in his transfiguration was not reflected, was not put on from without: it was essential to him, his own glory, and was identical with the glory of the Father.

figuration and preintimation that in due time he would identify himself with his people in a far more intimate and glorious way—that he would in grace and truth take up his abode with them, becoming one with them in human nature, and so fulfill the mighty prediction of his servant Isaiah, "Behold, a virgin shall conceive, and bear a son, and shall call his name Immanuel [With us God]" (Isa. 7 : 14).

We note a sort of progress in the manifestation of God to his people: first, his presence in the tabernacle; second, the incarnation of Christ; third, the indwelling of the Holy Spirit in believers; fourth, the descent of the New Jerusalem into the glorified earth.

HIGH PRIEST.

CHAPTER III

THE PRIESTHOOD

THE tabernacle, with its appointments, was of little practicable advantage to the mass of the Israelites, for it was to them inaccessible. They could only gaze on the dwelling-place of the Lord at a distance; they could not enter its sacred precincts. The Priesthood was the bond of union and medium of communication between the Holy One and the sinful people. The priest was the mediator between them.

I. THE UNIVERSALITY OF THE PRIESTLY OFFICE.

All religions are based on priesthood, for the office is essential to religion. Communion with God is impossible without it. Even Christianity has its glorious Priest, our Lord Jesus Christ; and all believers in him are kings and priests to God. Hidden and suffering priests they are now; glorified and royal priests they are to be.

II. PRIESTHOOD A REAL OFFICE.

Priesthood is a real office, definite and specific. It is needful to insist on this point, for the noble word "priesthood" has been misappropriated and misapplied, so that its intrinsic and peculiar import has been impaired. There is a certain literary slang abroad which talks of "the priests of nature," the "priests of science," and similar absurdities. The idea of priesthood, if priesthood is to have any real and definite meaning, can have no place whatever in science or literature or nature or anything of the kind. It belongs to the realm of grace, presupposing, as it does, sin and the divine purpose to remove it. Hugh Martin writes that he "would as soon think of transferring the language of geometry and algebra to botany, and talk of the hypothenuse of a flower and the square root of a tree, or the differential coëfficient of a convolvulus, as to speak of the priesthood of nature or letters." The priesthood, therefore, is an office, embracing very specific duties and functions.

III. THE TWO GREAT PRIESTS OF THE OLD TESTAMENT.

The two great priests of the Old Testament were Melchizedek and Aaron. No others that ever bore the name or discharged the office among the children of men rank with them, except, of course, our Lord; and of the two Melchizedek is the greater (Heb. 7 : 1-9). There are two reasons why they are to be considered the chiefs: First, because they are the *first* in their respective orders. Melchizedek was not only the head of his order, but he had no successor. It began and terminated with him (Heb. 7 : 3). The Levites and the common priests (the sons of Aaron) depended for their official existence on Aaron. Apart from him they could not be. Second, because the priesthood of Christ is typified by both. The office in both is summed up and completed in Christ. Indeed, it was in virtue of the reality of his priesthood that Melchizedek and Aaron were inducted into the office. They were called and consecrated in order that they might be types and shadows of Him in whom the priesthood has its origin, perfection, and permanence. In the Epistle to the Hebrews the priesthood as represented by them is combined and completed in the Lord Jesus. Christ is the antitype of both. But let it be carefully noted that *while he is of the order of Melchizedek he exercises the office after the pattern of Aaron.* In the execution of the office he perfects all that was done by Aaron, while at the same time, by divine decree, he is a priest forever after the order of Melchizedek.

IV. THE HIGH PRIEST IN ISRAEL.

The ministers of the sanctuary in the Mosaic economy were divided into three sections: *First,*

Levites. Properly, they were not priests, although they belonged to the priestly tribe. They were the servants and attendants of the priests proper. They were formed into three classes after the three sons of Levi—Gershon, Kohath, and Merari; and to each class was assigned a well-defined service. Their duties related to the taking down, transportation, and setting up of the tabernacle and its furniture. *Second,* the sons of Aaron. They were priests, consecrated to the office, in virtue of their relation to their father, *the priest.* "Take thou unto thee Aaron . . . and his sons, . . . that he may minister unto me in the priest's office" (Ex. 28 : 1). They ministered at the altar of sacrifice and in the holy place. They were also to teach the children of Israel the statutes of the Lord (Lev. 10 : 11; Deut. 33 : 10). *Third,* the high priest, whose office was the foundation of all the others. The Levites, when entering upon their functions, were first of all brought to Aaron, and "given unto him" (Num. 3 : 9). They were to keep *his* charge, and were to minister before *him.* The priests, sons of Aaron, and their father constituted the priestly family; but the sons were dependent for their official standing on their father. We might say without exaggeration that if the high priest could have performed all the priestly duties of the theocracy no others would have been associated with him.

1. *The High Priest's Dress.*

The high priest's dress was very elaborate, and is minutely described. It was deemed of so much importance that the Spirit has devoted an entire chapter to its description (Ex. 28). It appears to consist of seven parts, though some find, or try to find, eight; namely, the *ephod, breastplate, robe* of the ephod, *miter, broidered coat, girdle,* and *linen breeches,* or drawers. Only a few of the more prominent parts of this priestly attire may claim our attention. The dress was a very gorgeous one, one of "glory and beauty." Magnificent as is the papal attire on great occasions, attire which is but a counterfeit and admixture of that of Israel's high priest and of the pontifex maximus of pagan Rome, it sinks into comparative insignificance by the side of this splendid apparel. With its various parts of the richest material and of the most brilliant colors, with its golden bells, and miter or turban with its golden plate and solemn inscription, "Holiness to the Lord," it may be doubted whether anything more beautiful or imposing was ever worn.

(1) *The Ephod.* It was the outermost garment, being worn over the blue robe. It consisted of two parts, of which one covered the front, the other the back, and reached, it is thought, nearly to the knees. It was held to-

gether at the shoulders by pieces or straps, which were clasped firmly by two large onyx stones, and at the waist by the "curious girdle," which appears to have been a part of the ephod itself. The ephod was very costly and magnificent, being made of gold thread or wire, blue, purple, and scarlet. But its principal feature was the onyx gems that rested on the priest's shoulders. Indeed, the ephod was made for them, not they for it. These are thought to have been the sardonyx, the best kind of onyx, with its layers of black, white, and red. The names of the tribes were graven on them, six on the one stone, and six on the other. Thus the priest bore the names of the tribes of Israel on his shoulders when acting as the mediator of God and men.

(2) *The Breastplate.* It was made of the same material as the ephod, was four-square, doubling back upon itself so as to form a sort of pouch. It was fastened above and below to the ephod by threads of gold and ribbons of blue to rings of gold. It was filled with twelve precious stones, on each of which was engraved the name of a tribe. These gems were set in four rows, with three stones to a row. They thus corresponded to the twelve tribes, and they were probably arranged and engraved according to the divisions of the tribes in their camps. Israel

thus stood doubly represented by the high priest in the presence of God. On the brilliant stones that rested on his shoulders, their names were engraved according to their birth. Soltau gives them as follows (reading from right to left):

On the onyx on the left shoulder.	*On the onyx on the right shoulder.*
Gad.	Reuben.
Asher.	Simeon.
Issachar.	Levi.
Zebulun.	Judah.
Joseph.	Dan.
Benjamin.	Naphtali.

The stones in the breastplate were arranged according to the tribes, probably as follows:

The first row.

Carbuncle,	Topaz,	Sardius,
Zebulun.	Issachar.	Judah.

The second row.

Diamond,	Sapphire,	Emerald,
Gad.	Simeon.	Reuben.

The third row.

Amethyst,	Agate,	Ligure,
Benjamin.	Manasseh.	Ephraim.

The fourth row

Jasper,	Onyx,	Beryl,
Naphtali.	Asher.	Dan.

According to this arrangement of the stones in the breastplate, the place of honor is given Judah.

He stands at the head of the list. Similar was his position in the encampment. He faced the door of the tabernacle. So, too, in the enumeration of the "sealed ones" from among the tribes of Israel in Revelation 7 : 1-8, Judah takes precedence of the others. The reason of this distinction probably is, that Judah was the royal tribe, the one from whom was to spring the Messiah, David's princely Son and Lord.

(3) *The Miter and Golden Plate.* This formed the head-dress of the high priest. Josephus tells us that it was "not a conical cap, but a sort of crown, made of thick linen swathes." It was totally unlike the tiara of the pope or the miter of a bishop. It was in reality a species of turban. The color was white, and its only ornamentation was the gold plate, with its blue ribbon or fillet. The gold plate was the most conspicuous and most significant feature of the miter. Its position made it "the culminating point of the whole priestly attire."[1] The plate bore the inscription, "Holiness to the Lord." It taught that the very highest crown and the truest excellence of all religion and ceremony is holiness. It set this prime truth before the eyes of all Israel. It taught the high priest himself not to rest on outward forms, to put no trust in mere rites, but to

[1] Kalisch.

be holy in himself, both personally and as holding the highest office in the theocracy. To all it announced, "Holiness becometh thine house, O Lord, for ever" (Ps. 93 : 5); "Follow . . . holiness, without which no man shall see the Lord" (Heb. 12 : 14).

(4) *Urim and Thummim.* It appears from Exodus 28 : 30, that these mysterious objects were placed within the breastplate. At any rate, they are described in such fashion as to leave little doubt but that they were distinct from the breastplate, and something additional to it. What they were is extremely uncertain. Very much that is written of them is pure conjecture. But as Scripture connects the ephod with the use of teraphim, some sober interpreters are of opinion that the Urim and Thummim resembled these objects, if they were not identical with them (Judg. 17: 5 ; 18 : 14, 17, 20 ; Hos. 3: 4). It seems quite probable that the teraphim were not always objects of idolatrous worship, nor were they images precisely. The words "Urim" and "Thummim" signify *lights* and *perfections.* By means of them in some inexplicable manner God's will was made known to the priest.

2. *The High Priest a Type of Christ.*

That the high priest was a remarkable type of Christ, in his office, functions, and sacerdotal dress, is certain. The Epistle to the Hebrews puts this beyond question. In that scripture Jesus receives the name, our "High Priest," and he fulfills the duties of the office after the pattern of Aaron. Indeed, it is in virtue of the transcendent fact of Christ's priestly office that Aaron's was instituted in Israel; Christ's reflects backward and gives to that of Aaron all the efficacy and meaning that it possessed. In Revelation 1 the glorified Saviour is seen by John as clothed with priestly robes that strikingly resemble those of Aaron.

Aaron was Israel's representative before God. His office, his bearing the names of the twelve tribes on his shoulders and on his breast, and the legend over his forehead, "Holiness to the Lord," attest this fact. In his priestly character he stood for the whole nation. When God was pleased with him, he was pleased with the whole nation. In the sight of God he was Israel. The inscription on the gold plate of the miter was not designed so much to denote what he was to be in his individual person and private life: it was public and official; it pertained more especially to his office as the mediator between God and the people. Israel stood at a distance from God because of sin; even their holy things were full of defilement and pollution. They needed a priest who, by virtue of divine appointment, could act in their behalf and mediate for them with God. And this the high priest was. As mediator he bore the tribes into the very presence of the Holy One. Our High Priest, Jesus Christ, bears his people into God's presence. On his mighty shoulders they rest. On his heart they are found, loved, cherished, guarded, and cared for, with a patience and an affection which nothing can extinguish. They need never fear that he will grow weary of the burden, or displace them from his shoulders or his breast, for he is the merciful and faithful High Priest, who can be touched with a feeling of our infirmities (Heb. 4 : 15, 16). He is the Lord our righteousness, and in him we become the righteousness of God, for he is the perfectly Holy One.

3. *The Functions of the High Priest.*

The functions of the high priest and of the priestly family are minutely prescribed in the law. In the institution of the office the Lord's words to Moses were, "Take thou unto thee Aaron thy brother, and his sons with him, from among the children of Israel, that he may *minister unto me in the priest's office*" (Ex. 28 : 1). Their duties were strictly religious. They had no political power conferred upon them. Their services, their dependent position, and the way in which they were sustained, precluded them from exercising any undue influence in the affairs of the nation. It is true that in process of time the office degenerated and sank into such corruption as to become a thing of barter and bribe, and a tool in the hands of unscrupulous rulers; but as originally instituted, the priesthood in Israel was not a caste, nor a hierarchy, nor a political factor, but a divinely appointed medium of communication between God and the people.

The Hebrew priests in no wise interfered with the individual conscience. In this respect they differed totally from heathen priests, and from those now found in Roman Catholicism. It is the main business of Rome to thrust its priestly power and craft between the souls of men and God, to seize upon the conscience and to mold and manipulate it to its own interests. Probably there is no politico-religious system on earth that more effectively dominates and perverts the human conscience than that of Rome. Israel's priests were not *father confessors*. The Hebrew worshiper of his own free will and according to his own ability confessed his sins to God and laid his hand on the head of his sacrifice. His conscience was left perfectly free and untrammeled.

There were certain duties which were peculiar

to the high priest. He only could wear the "garments for glory and for beauty." To him alone it pertained to enter the most holy place and to sprinkle the blood of the sin-offering on the mercy-seat. To him alone it belonged to represent the congregation before the Lord as mediator, and to receive the divine communications. He was to be ceremonially pure and holy. God is holy, before whom the high priest served as the representative of the people, and therefore must he be also. He must be physically perfect. Any defect or deformity disqualified a member of the priestly family to perform the duties of the office (Lev. 21: 17-21). The law spoke with the utmost precision as to the domestic relations of the high priest. He could marry neither a widow, nor a divorced woman, nor one polluted, nor a harlot; only a virgin of his own people, a Hebrew of pure extraction, could become his wife (Lev. 21: 14, 15). Nor was he to come in contact with *death*. He must not rend his clothes, nor defile himself even for his father or his mother (Lev. 21: 10, 11). His sons might defile themselves for their kin, but the high priest must not. For he was the representative of *life*. Death did not exist for him, in so far as he was a priest. God is the Ever Living, the Life-Giving; and his priest, who had "the crown of the anointing oil of his God upon him," had to do with life alone. There is deep significance in the miracle of Aaron's rod that budded and bare almonds (Num. 17). It was a visible sign of the legitimacy of Aaron's priesthood and a confirmation of it, and a symbol of its vitality and fruitfulness. The twelve rods that represented the tribes were dead sticks of wood, and remained dead; Aaron's alone exhibited life and produced blossoms and fruit. It was symbolical of his priesthood, which correlated itself with life, and had nothing to do with death.

All this looked forward to a Greater Priest and to a more perfect office. What the high priest was ceremonially and symbolically, the Lord Jesus is intrinsically and divinely. By his incarnation he "wedded himself with our nature," that as a man he might act for men, and offer a sacrifice in the nature that had sinned. But Scripture is very careful to explain that the humanity he assumed was absolutely holy and pure. The angel announced to Mary, his virgin mother, that "that holy thing which shall be born of thee shall be called the Son of God" (Luke 1:35). "Who did no sin, neither was guile found in his mouth" (I. Pet. 2:22). "For such an High Priest became us, who is holy, harmless, undefiled, separate from sinners, and made higher than the heavens" (Heb. 7 : 26). Although as to his humanity Christ was descended from a long line of impure ancestors, yet he brought not the slightest taint or stain into the world with him. Although he long .conversed with sinful men and grappled with fierce temptations, yet he contracted no blur, nor breath of guilt. He could touch the leper and the unclean, and yet remain undefiled, for he was undefilable. So also his priesthood is both vital and vitalizing. In him was life, for he is the Prince and principle of all life, and he came to give life, even the more abundant life (John 1 : 4; 10 : 10). He was made a Priest "after the power of an endless life" (Heb. 7 : 16); "wherefore he is able also to save them to the uttermost that come unto God by him, seeing he ever liveth to make intercession for them" (Heb. 7 : 25).

V. THE NATURE OF THE PRIESTLY OFFICE.

Since the Lord Jesus Christ is the antitype of Aaron and accomplished perfectly all that the latter foreshadowed, the inquiry is pertinent and important: What was the character of the Aaronic office? What did it involve?

1. *It implies choice.* Not only was the office of divine institution, but the priest himself was appointed of God to the office. "For every high

priest taken from among men is ordained for men in things pertaining to God. . . . And no man taketh this honour unto himself, but he that is called of God, as was Aaron" (Heb. 5 : 1, 4). The priest was not self-appointed, much less was he elected by the people. Divine selection severed him from those for whom he was to act. "So also Christ glorified not himself to be made an High Priest; but he that said unto him, Thou art my Son, to-day have I begotten thee" (Heb. 5 : 5). Our glorious Priest came not into the world unsent. He received his commission and his authority from God, the fountain of all sovereignty. At the opening of his ministry he said, "He hath anointed me . . .; he hath sent me" (Luke 4 : 18). He came bearing heavenly credentials, and what he did and suffered he had a divine warrant for from the God of glory.

2. *It implies the principle of representation.* The institution of the office (Ex. 28, 29) was God's gracious provision for a people at a distance from him, who needed one to appear in the divine presence in their behalf. The high priest was to act for men in things pertaining to God, to "offer both gifts and sacrifices for sins" (Heb. 5 : 1), "to make reconciliation for the sins of the people" (Heb. 2 : 17). Accordingly, he was the mediator between the offended Lord and the guilty people.

"The high priest," says Vitringa, "represented the whole people. All Israelities were reckoned as being in him. The prerogative held by him belonged to the whole of them (Ex. 19 : 6), but on this account it was transferred to him because it was impossible that all Israelites should keep themselves holy as became the priests of Jehovah." That the high priest did represent the entire congregation in his official character appears, first, from his bearing the tribal names upon his shoulders and over his heart; second, because his committing heinous sin involved the people in his guilt—"If the anointed priest shall sin so as to bring guilt on the people" (Lev. 4 : 3, R. V.). The version of the Septuagint is, "to make the people sin." The anointed priest was the high priest; no other can be meant in this place. When he sinned, the people sinned. His official action was reckoned as their action. The whole nation was involved in the transgression of their representative. The converse appears to be just as true. The official acts of the high priest were reckoned as done by the congregation. Such is the legitimate inference from the transactions on the Day of Expiation (Lev. 16). It was for the congregation as a corporate body that Aaron carried the blood into the holy of holies and sprinkled it on and before the mercy-seat; for the nation also he symbolically transferred the sins of Israel to the head of the scapegoat, which bore them away into a land of forgetfulness. "Every high priest . . . is ordained for men" (ὑπὲρ ἀνθρώπων, for their benefit and in their place) (Heb. 5:1). The plain teaching of this text is, that the high priest acted in behalf of the people —represented them.

The representative principle in the priesthood of Israel was symbolical and most significant. It set forth the mighty truth, so essential in Christianity, that the true Priest, of whom Aaron was but a dim shadow, a faithful but faint picture, sustains to his people relations far more intimate and real than did the high priest to Israel; that the Mediator of the new covenant stands as the representative of believers—is their Surety and Redeemer (Rom. 5:15-19; II. Cor. 5:21; I. Pet. 3:18). By virtue of Christ's representative character the Scriptures affirm that whatever he did as Saviour and Mediator is reckoned as having been done by believers. Did he die? They all died with him (II. Cor. 5:14). Was he quickened from the dead? They are said to be quickened together with Christ, and are raised up with him, and with him they are seated in the heavenlies (Eph. 2:5, 6). In fact, so complete is the identity between him and them that Paul exhorts the saints who have died to sin in Christ now to reckon themselves to be indeed dead unto sin, but alive unto God in Christ Jesus (Rom. 6 : 11). The Bible recognizes two great heads of our race, Adam and Christ. Both are representative persons; the acts of each reach far beyond himself. The act of Adam ruined humanity. The act of Christ in grace on the cross redeems and restores to eternal life all who trust in him. The one is as certainly a representative as the other. It is this truth which lies at the foundation of the atonement, and it is this alone which adequately explains the history of the race, the Mosaic economy, and God's ways with this rebellious world.

3. *It implies the offering of sacrifice.* Nothing can be clearer than the teaching of Scripture as to the prominence of this priestly function. It is the chief duty of a priest to reconcile men to God by atoning for their sins; and this he effects by means of sacrifice—bloodshedding. "For every high priest . . . is ordained for men" (Heb. 5 : 1), that he may offer both "gifts and sacrifices" (Heb. 8 : 3). He would be no priest who should have nothing to offer. By the expression "gifts and sacrifices," is probably meant both the bloodless and bloody offerings of the law. Both kinds were presented to God on the Day of Expiation

(Num. 29 : 7-11). This the high priest did *for men*—in their behalf and in their stead. Besides, it was the high priest who sprinkled the blood of the sin-sacrifice on the mercy-seat, thus symbolically covering the sins of the people from the sight of Jehovah, who dwelt between the cherubim (Ps. 80 : 1). It was he, likewise, who marked with the same blood the horns of both altars, that, as one has truthfully said, the red sign of propitiation might be lifted up toward Jehovah.

That the action of the high priest in Israel was typical of our Lord's sacrificial action in behalf of his people, must be apparent to every reader of the Bible. In Hebrews 8 : 3 (R. V.) we read, "Wherefore it is necessary that this *high priest* also have somewhat to offer." Why the necessity? Because otherwise he could not be a priest, for this is the distinctive duty of a priest. A priest without a sacrifice is like a king without a kingdom, or a prophet without a message or a mission. In verse 2 Christ is called "a minister of the sanctuary"—an appropriate designation of his exalted position. His offering as far exceeds the Levitical sacrifices as his glorious person transcends that of a mere man; for it was himself (Heb. 7: 27), it was his own body (Heb. 10: 10), his own blood (Heb. 9: 12), that he presented. His priestly ministry as far excels that of Aaron as does the heavenly sanctuary the earthly.

4. *It implies intercession.* This also is an element of the priestly office. In the ministry of the high priest it is not so expressly set forth as are his other functions, but it is certainly implied and involved therein. For intercession is grounded in sacrifice. There can be no effective advocacy on behalf of the guilty until the guilt is expiated and removed. The sprinkling of the blood of the sin-offering on the mercy-seat served to cover the guilt from the face of God, and at the same time it was an appeal to him to forgive and bless his people according to the covenant promise. So we read that after Aaron had thus sprinkled the blood he came forth from the sanctuary to bless Israel (Lev. 9 : 22-24 ; cf. Num. 6 : 22-27 ; I. Chr. 23 : 13 ; Deut. 21 : 5). Aaron "lifted up his hands—the very hands that had been wet with blood—and blessed the people. It was as if he was pouring over them all the grace and peace that flow from the blood of Jesus."[1] He well could bless the chosen of the Lord, since atonement had been made for their guilt, reconciliation effected, and peace established.

The Scriptures expressly combine Christ's intercession and his sacrificial death. In his interces-

[1] Bonar.

sional prayer (John 17) the *place* he takes is beyond the cross. He contemplates his work as finished; and on the ground of accomplished redemption he presents his petitions to the Father. So, also, in I. John 2 : 1, 2, his advocacy is joined with his propitiation. So, too, in Hebrews 9 : 24 he is said to appear before the face of God for us (see Greek). He presents himself before God as our representative. His perfect manhood, his official character, and his finished work plead for us before the throne of God. All that the Son of God as incarnate is, and all that he did on earth, he is and did for us; so that the infinite dignity of his person and the infinite perfection of his redemptive work combine and unite in his glorious intercession. If on the ground of the blood of bulls and goats the high priest in Israel could thrice repeat the name and the blessing of Jehovah upon the chosen people, how much more efficacious and availing is the plea of Jesus, who pleads the precious merits of his own blood, as of a lamb without blemish and without spot? "Wherefore he is able also to save them to the uttermost that come unto God by him, seeing he ever liveth to make intercession for them" (Heb. 7: 25). "To the uttermost" (εἰς τὸ παντελὲς)—completely, perfectly, out and out. And so Paul could fling abroad his mighty challenge: "Who shall lay any thing to the charge of God's elect? ... Who is he that condemneth? It is Christ that died, yea rather, that is risen again, who is even at the right hand of God, who also maketh intercession for us" (Rom. 8 : 33, 34).

5. *It implies action toward God.* Priesthood, with all its accompanying acts, is directed primarily to him. "For every high priest taken from among men is ordained for men in things *pertaining* to God" (τὰ πρὸς τὸν θεόν) (Heb. 5 : 1). Its object is God. It looks and acts toward him. It propitiates him, and satisfies his justice. It intercedes with him. It seals his covenant love. It gives effect to his eternal purpose and grace. For it removes every obstruction to the outflowing of his favor and blessing.

It is remarkable that this very expression— "things pertaining to God"—is applied to Christ —"Wherefore in all things it behoved him to be made like unto his brethren, that he might be a merciful and faithful High Priest in things pertaining to God, to make reconciliation for the sins of the people" (Heb. 2: 17). Here is the great Archetype. The heavenly High Priest makes the true propitiation for the sins of his people; meets every requirement in their room, whether of law, or justice, or death; satisfies every divine claim against them; reconciles them to God; establishes the friendship with God which their sins had utterly forfeited, and satisfies God with respect to them most blessedly and perfectly.

We may here sum up some of the perfections of Christ's priesthood. As a priest

(1) He is appointed of God (Heb. 5 : 5).

(2) He is consecrated with an oath (Heb. 7 : 20-22).

(3) He is sinless (Heb. 7 : 26).

(4) His priesthood is unchangeable (Heb. 7 : 23, 24).

(5) His offering is perfect and final (Heb. 9 : 25-28).

(6) His intercession is all-prevailing (Heb. 7 : 25).

(7) As God-man Mediator he is qualified to act both for God and in behalf of men (Heb. 1, 2).

VI. THE CONSECRATION OF AARON AND HIS SONS.

The record of this significant transaction is found in Exodus 29; Leviticus 8. The first of these chapters gives specific directions as to the consecration; the second records its performance after the tabernacle was erected. Brief notes on the solemn act are appended.

1. *Aaron and his sons shared in the consecration,*

for together they formed the priestly family. But the high priest takes the precedence and has the preëminence, for he is chief, the sons being subordinate and dependent on him for their official standing. Typically, they represent Christ and believers who constitute the household of God, the royal and priestly family, of whom our Lord is the glorious Head, "the first-born among many brethren" (Rom. 8: 29).

2. *Their Washing with Water.* This was the first step in the ceremony of their consecration. Aaron and his sons were washed at the same time. It was probably at the laver that they were washed. It was indispensable that they should be ceremonially clean. Nothing could be done until all defilement had been removed. His absolution rendered the high priest symbolically, what Christ was intrinsically, holy.

3. *The investiture* of Aaron followed the washing with water (Lev. 8: 7-9). It should be observed, that at this point in the proceeding the high priest parts company with his sons. His robing and anointing preceded that of his sons. They had to wait until the sin-sacrifice had been offered before they received the holy oil, though their robing appears to have succeeded the anointing of their father (v. 13).

4. *The Anointing of the High Priest.* It was

with the precious oil described in Exodus 30: 22-33 that this prime feature in the consecration was consummated. For the making of it God himself gave a minute prescription, and solemnly forbade any imitation of it, or its use by any private person as a mere unguent, precisely as he did in the case of the holy incense. It is called "an holy anointing oil unto me" (Ex. 30: 31). It belonged in some peculiar sense to God, and was to be employed only as he directed. The reason for these specific orders it is not difficult to discover. The holy anointing oil was designed to be the emblem of the gift and grace of the Holy Spirit (II. Cor. 1: 21; I. John 2: 20, 27). And our Great High Priest was anointed with the Holy Ghost, accomplishing thus as the Antitype what was symbolically done in the person of Israel's first high priest (Acts 4: 27; 10: 38).

Note (1): Moses *poured* of the anointing oil on Aaron's head (Lev. 8: 12). When he anointed the tabernacle and its furniture he *sprinkled* the oil. In the case of the high priest there was a profusion, an abundance, in which neither the tent nor Aaron's sons shared. To this reference is made in Psalm 133: 2: "It is like the precious ointment upon the head, that ran down upon the beard, even Aaron's beard; that went down to the skirts of his garments." So copious was it that the priest's person from head to foot was touched by and brought under the power of the sacred oil. All this strikingly foreshadowed the fullness of the gift of the Holy Spirit to the Lord Jesus that he might be set apart and qualified for his great mission. Long before his advent it had been predicted that he should be anointed with the Spirit for his work (Isa. 61: 1-3). In one of his first public discourses, that at Nazareth (Luke 4), Jesus read this Messianic promise and announced its fulfillment that day. It was in the power of the Spirit that he spoke; so we read in John 3: 34—"For he whom God hath sent speaketh the words of God: for God giveth not the Spirit by measure unto him." Whether in the second member of this verse the word "God" be omitted (with Revised Version, Westcott and Hort), or retained (with *Textus Receptus*, Vulgate, etc.), the meaning undoubtedly is, the gift of the Spirit in an unlimited degree to the Son of God. As Aaron was consecrated as a priest unto God and inducted into his office by being anointed with the holy oil, so and much more was the Lord Jesus anointed and introduced to his public life as the High Priest of our profession by the unmeasured gift of the Spirit.

Note (2): Aaron was anointed before the bloody sacrifices were offered; his sons not until afterward. The record distinctly relates that it was not until after they had been marked by the blood that they were anointed (Ex. 29 : 20, 21; Lev. 8 : 24, 30). Now this is most remarkable and suggestive. Vivid pictures of profound realities are here drawn for us. Long before the cross Jesus was anointed with the Holy Ghost, as we have just seen. At his baptism the Spirit descended upon him in visible form, and the Father testified to his satisfaction with him. John the Baptist bore witness that this was the sign whereby he was to recognize the Messiah (John 1 : 33, 34). But the disciples, who are the antitypes of the sons of Aaron, did not then receive him. John most emphatically affirms that "this spake he of the Spirit, which they that believed on him were to receive : for the Spirit was not yet given ; because Jesus was not yet glorified" (John 7 : 39, R. V.). The reference is certainly to the outpouring of the Spirit on the day of Pentecost. Of course, all know that the Old Testament attests the presence and work of the Spirit from the beginning of our race, for it has always been his office to apply the redemption of Christ to believers. But in a fuller way, with an outpouring beyond anything ever experienced before, was the Spirit to be given after Jesus was glorified. Christ himself said that it was expedient that he should go away, else the Comforter would not come (John 16 : 7-15); that on his withdrawal from the world another Comforter would take his place: "another"—One instead of himself; One like himself; One that would be to the disciples all that he had been, and even more, as Jesus seems to intimate.

It was not till the Saviour was glorified that the Holy Spirit came with power upon the church. Peter affirms that what the multitude witnessed on the day of Pentecost was the result, the blessed and glorious fruit, of Christ's death and resurrection (Acts 2). "Being therefore by the right hand of God exalted, and having received of the Father the promise of the Holy Ghost, he hath *poured forth* this, which ye see and hear" (Acts 2 : 33, R.V.).

Note (3): Aaron received a greater unction than his sons. The holy oil was poured on his head, and his whole person was perfumed with its fragrance. Jesus was likewise anointed with the oil of gladness above his fellows (Heb. 1 : 9). In all things and everywhere Christ has the preeminence. His infinite grace associates him with his brethren, brings him near them, and they in turn were brought near him. Nevertheless, he is above them. They received the Spirit according to the measure of their ability; but he without measure. Our High Priest is first, and always first.

5. *The Bloodshedding, and the Application of the Blood to the Priests.* It is noteworthy that the whole round of Levitical sacrifices was observed in the consecration of the priests. The ceremony began with the sin-offering; the altar must first be purified. That is, there can be no progress in the rite until sin is judged and put away. Next, a burnt-offering was presented. Propitiation is succeeded by the "savour of a sweet smell." Further, the ram of consecration was offered, which corresponds to the peace-offering, and this was followed by the meat-offering.

The blood being shed, it was applied to the high priest and his sons. On the tip of the right ear, on the thumb of the right hand, and on the great toe of the right foot, was the blood put by Moses (Lev. 8 : 24). That is, his whole career as priest was brought under the power of the blood. He had a blood-stained ear, that he might hear and obey the divine communications; a blood-stained hand, that he might execute the services of the sanctuary; and a blood-stained foot, to tread the courts of the Lord's house. The blood here, as everywhere else, is the foundation for sinners and saints alike in all their relations with God.

6. *The Anointing of Aaron's Sons.* It followed the application of the blood to their persons; and it consisted of the holy oil and the blood from the altar (Lev. 8 : 30). Just what is meant by the "blood which was upon the altar," it is difficult to determine. Clear it is, however, that it could not have been that of the sin-offering, for whatever object that touched, whether garment or vessel, it defiled, because it was blood loaded with sin (Lev. 6 : 27, 28). It must have been either that of the burnt-offering or of the ram of consecration — most probably the latter. Moses mixed the oil and blood and sprinkled it on Aaron and on his garments; on his sons, also, and on their garments. For, although Aaron in his highpriestly character was an eminent type of Christ, he was, nevertheless, like his sons, a sinner, and needed purification no less than they. Jesus, the Archetypal Priest, was supremely holy, and required no offering for himself. After the sin- and burnt-offerings and the ram of consecration had been presented, the sons were anointed with the oil and the blood. Shadows of good things are passing before us in their divine order. It was after Jesus died and rose again that the Holy Spirit was given to the disciples and the church. The promise of the gift of the Spirit could only be fulfilled when the mighty sin-sacrifice by the

Son of God at Calvary had been accomplished, and Jesus was glorified (John 7 : 38, 39 ; 16 : 7).

7. *Retirement of the Priestly Family at the Conclusion of the Consecration Ceremonies Proper* (Lev. 8 : 31-36). For seven days they were to remain within the tabernacle enclosure. On pain of death they were forbidden to go forth from thence. Of the peace- and meat-offerings they were to eat in the meanwhile. No other but priests could partake of them. Then when the "eighth day" (Lev. 9 : 1) arrived, they were to come forth, offer sacrifices for the people, and bless the people in the great name of Jehovah (Lev. 9 : 22, 23). "And the glory of the Lord appeared unto all the people." The shadows of good things are again passing before us. One is reminded of the quiet retirement of the disciples and their assembly in the upper room at Jerusalem during the interval between Jesus' ascension and the day of Pentecost. Patiently and unitedly they waited and prayed that the promise of the enduement with power might be fulfilled. Fifty days after the most amazing Passover ever observed, the Passover when Jesus was crucified, the promise of the Spirit was accomplished, "and they were all filled with the Holy Ghost, and began to speak with other tongues, as the Spirit gave them utterance."

The eighth day was fully come. Generally, the eighth day corresponds with the first day of the week, the Lord's day. The fiftieth day, that is, the day of Pentecost, answers likewise to the eighth day, the Lord's day. And on that fiftieth day the glory of the Lord appeared to the disciples at Jerusalem as it had appeared long before at the consecration of Aaron and his sons (Lev. 9 : 23). The two events are related as prediction and fulfillment. The one is the shadow, the other the reality.

8. *Priestly Blessing of the Chosen People* (Lev. 9: 23). The closing act in connection with the consecration of the priests was a most impressive and instructive one. The record of this act is in the ninth chapter of Leviticus, and is worthy of a more careful study than can here be given it. Its more prominent features only are noticed.

At the end of the seven days' retirement the first priestly act of Aaron was performed. It was the eighth day. By direction of Moses, the whole round of sacrifices was observed — the sin-, burnt-, meat-, and peace-offerings were presented, first, for Aaron himself and his priestly family, and second, for the congregation. The order observed in this first great official sacrifice is worthy of attention. The sin-offering in both instances was first made; then followed the sweet-savor sacrifices, which were for acceptance and worship. Guilt must first be dealt with and removed in a way in strict accordance with the justice of God; then worship, communion, and peace may be enjoyed. Bonar is of opinion that these offerings were made at the time of the morning sacrifice. Afterward, Moses and Aaron retired into the tabernacle (v. 23). It was Aaron's first entrance into the sanctuary in his character as high priest. During this retirement Moses, as representative of Jehovah, committed to Aaron the care of the things within the tabernacle, as he had already given him the charge of all the sacrifices of the court.[1]

Here again the shadow of good things to come passes before us. When our Great High Priest had finished his sacrificial work at Calvary, he too retired into the presence of the Father, and to him was given all power in heaven and in earth (Matt. 28: 18). He now is invested with all mediatorial authority, as the perfected Captain of our salvation (Heb. 2: 10), to administer the affairs of the sanctuary. He is there now, managing the interests of his people and his cause, preparing for them the many mansions, preparing for it the most stupendous victory. "The Father . . . hath given all things into his hand." No

[1] Rawlinson, Bonar.

name is surrounded with such splendor. Our
Priest on high has no superior and no rival. No
sphere, however high or distant, is exempted from
his control; no creature, however mighty or exalted, has a coördinate jurisdiction. We may
well trust him, for his power is more than a
match for all our adversaries; his mercy and
love are pledged in our behalf.

The people remained in the court waiting the
reappearance of the law-giver and the priest. We
know that this period of expectancy was one of
no little anxiety, at least on other occasions.
When the high priest entered the most holy
place on the Day of Expiation, the congregation
waited his return with earnestness and deep
solicitude, for his reappearance was at once the
signal and the assurance that the atonement
which he had gone within to present before the
mysterious Presence was accepted. When our
High Priest went up on high, the two heavenly
visitants said to the disciples: "Ye men of
Galilee, why stand ye gazing up into heaven?
this same Jesus, which is taken up from you
into heaven, shall so come in like manner as ye
have seen him go into heaven" (Acts 1: 11).
And the attitude of believers now with respect to
this transcendent event, the greatest the world is
ever to see since our Lord's ascension, is to be

precisely that of Israel of old; waiting, watching, expecting, until he shall come again.

At length (how long after they had gone within we do not know), Moses and Aaron came forth again, and "blessed the people: and the glory of the Lord appeared unto all the people." It was no doubt the priestly blessing which was pronounced—"The Lord bless thee, and keep thee; the Lord make his face shine upon thee, and be gracious unto thee; the Lord lift up his countenance upon thee, and give thee peace" (Num. 6 : 24-26). In all this we see the very figure and outlines of the Lord's second coming, who shall appear the second time to them that look for him without sin unto salvation (Heb. 9 : 28). His promise is, "A little while, and ye shall not see me: and again, a little while, and ye shall see me; because I go to the Father" (John 16 : 16). To many of the saints the little while has been long and weary, for amid disappointments, blasted hopes, sorrows, and tears they have waited for his return. Earth has been a sort of prison to them, and the time that of night. But the night will pass round, the morning break, the blissful morning of his coming, and then the time that seemed so long in the waiting will appear as only a "little while" for the gladness and joy which they shall have.

It was the eighth day; and the glory of the Lord appeared unto all the people; and all the people shouted and fell on their faces. It will be the eighth day indeed, the Millennial Day, when our Lord shall come again. What a shout of ecstasy shall burst from his people! Can we not pray with the saintly Andrew Bonar: "And soon, soon come forth again! yea, even before we have slept with our fathers, if it seem good in thy sight; come forth to bless us, and to receive the shout of multitudes adoring and confessing that thou art Lord alone!"

All through this marvelous transaction in the wilderness so long ago we see, we cannot but see, type and antitype most wondrously matching and combining. The spiritually minded need no other proof than this, and such as this, to be profoundly persuaded of the inspiration of the books of Moses. Face to face with this manifest prescience of the Spirit of God, how incredible to the believer, how steeped with silly nonsense, is the hypothesis of the higher criticism, that Leviticus is the fraudulent product of impostors, who wrote it at the close of the Babylonian exile, and in the name of Moses to give it authority and currency with the Hebrew people!

CHAPTER IV

THE SACRIFICES OFFERED AT THE BRAZEN ALTAR

GENERAL OBSERVATIONS
(Lev. 1-7)

IN the appointments and ordinances of the tabernacle there are certain great principles which underlie the whole, without a knowledge of which the entire service becomes meaningless, if not puerile. Before passing to the study of the offerings made on the brazen altar, let us state some of these principles and truths.

1. *The Prevalence of Sin.* All sacrifice is grounded in the fact of sin. The Levitical legislation is wholly occupied with it. Sin, man's sin,—sin before and after justification, is the secret of Judaism, and the secret likewise of the gospel. Face to face with the Mosaic ritual we are face to face with sin. Guilt, universal, defiling, excisive, destructive, is the primal cause of God's provision in the offerings.

2. *God's Holiness.* He is represented throughout all Scripture as being totally unable to tolerate

sin, even in his people. He is of purer eyes than to behold evil, and he cannot look upon iniquity (Hab. 1: 13). He may pity and love, as assuredly he does, but he cannot connive at sin. He cannot slur it over, or treat it with indifference. "Shall not the Judge of all the earth do right?" While God is God, sin must receive its just deserts. His holiness, his righteousness, his truth,—every attribute of his being, demands the infliction of the penalty due to sin. In the sacrificing priest and the fire which consumes the sacrifice; in the blood which streams from the dying victim; in the ashes and the water; in the incense and the prayer; in the distance between himself and the people; in the darkness and loneliness of the most holy place, his dwelling, we have the solemn portraiture of God's holiness and justice—his infinite purpose, impelled by his very nature, to punish sin, to expunge and blot it out, and annihilate it forever.

3. *God's Remedy for Man's Sin—Bloodshedding.* This is the central idea in the offerings. They were God's gracious provision to meet the requirements of his own character and man's need. In the Old Testament the most general term for "sacrifice" is *corban*. Professor Cave is of the opinion that this word was employed in the Law to describe the "genus, of which sacrifices of all

kinds were species." "It is expressly predicated of the burnt-offering, the peace-offering, the thank-offering, and the votive-offering, the sin-offering, the trespass-offering, the Passover, the meat-offering, the sacrifice of the Nazarite, the whole range of national sacrifices, the first-fruits, and even offerings made to Jehovah of the spoils of battle. In short, *corban* is the word which expresses what every form of sacrifice shared in common."

The important thing is to ascertain the precise meaning of this word *corban*. Happily, we are not left to lexicons or commentaries in the matter. The Bible itself furnishes the needed information. Our Lord defines it as it was understood and employed by the Jews at his time: "If a man shall say to his father or his mother, That wherewith thou mightest have been profited by me is Corban, that is to say, Given *to God;* ye no longer suffer him to do aught for his father or his mother" (Mark 7 : 11, 12, R.V.). This settles the import of this sacrificial term. *Corban* is a gift to God—something devoted to him, and therefore sacred. A sacrifice in the Levitical sense was an offering made to Jehovah. The chief element in it was that of propitiation, or atonement. It was presented for the specific end of propitiating the Lord as touching sins committed. That this is

THE SACRIFICES AT THE BRAZEN ALTAR 131

the essential idea in the sacrifices of Leviticus no fair-minded man can for a moment doubt. God's righteousness and man's sin : the blood shed at the brazen altar, and the body of the victim burned with fire, that satisfaction to divine justice may be rendered by the offender in the person of a substitute,—this vital truth lies at the foundation of all the offerings of the Mosaic system.

4. *The Parties to the Sacrifice.* These are the priest, the offerer, and the offering. The priest acts as a mediator. In his official character the priest and priestly action imply God and a sinner, who are to be brought together, and a relationship of favor and peace established between them. The offering points unmistakably to sin committed and to the absolute need of expiation. The offerer is the offending party, who in every bloody sacrifice is regarded as identified with his offering. The life of the animal is substituted for the life of the man, and, it being reckoned guilty through the symbolical transference of his sins to it by the imposition of his hands on its head, dies in his place.

5. *The offerings of Leviticus are pictures of the one supreme offering of the Lord Jesus Christ.* He is the sum and substance of them all. As no one of them could be anything like an adequate type of him, five were instituted in order to set forth

as in a kind of object-lesson the perfection of his sacrifice. In the application of sacrificial types all the features that distinguish them are found to unite and combine in the person and work of the Lord Jesus. He is at once the Priest, the Victim, and the Offerer. In his death there is priestly action; the offering he presents is himself; and in it all he and those for whom he acts are identified. Thus did he conceive of his work—"And for their sakes I sanctify [*consecrate*—a distinctly priestly term] myself, that they themselves also may be sanctified in truth" (John 17 : 19, R. V.).

6. *The offerings described in Leviticus 1-7 are divided into two classes;* namely, first, the "sweet-savour" offerings, which are three, to wit: Burnt-, Meat-, and Peace-offerings; and second, those designed more especially for the expiation of sin, namely, the Sin- and Trespass-offerings. The meat-offering was vegetable; all the others were animal sacrifices. The victims were selected from the class of clean animals appropriated for the support of human life. They were taken from those that stand nearest to man, and on which human life largely depends for subsistence, as the ox, the sheep, and the goat. They were to be free from all blemish. The law was very strict on this point (Lev. 22 : 20-25). Even in the meat-offering the finest flour was to be used. This physical

perfection was typical of the freedom from all sin of Him who is the fulfillment of all the rites established by Moses.

These two classes of offerings differ from each other both as to design and as to the ceremonial observed. The "sweet-savour" offerings were for acceptance and worship, the sin-offerings for expiation of sin. In the first, guilt is not the main idea—sin is not even mentioned; in the second, guilt is most prominent. In the former we see God's satisfaction, and communion with him as founded on his satisfaction, preëminently set forth; in the latter we see God's judgment executed on the victim as charged with the sin of the offerer. So, likewise, there is a difference in the ceremonial observed in the two classes. The burnt-offering, the chief of its class, was wholly consumed on the brazen altar, while only a small portion of the sin-sacrifices was burned on the altar, the body of the victim being consumed without the camp (Lev. 4 : 11, 12).

7. Another preliminary observation to be made respects the *order* in which the sacrifices are arranged in these chapters of Leviticus. It will be observed that the sweet-savor offerings are first described, and the sin-sacrifices follow these. But the former undoubtedly were presented for acceptance with God, and for worship, whereas

the latter had to do exclusively with expiation of sin. But in the order of nature the sin-sacrifices take the precedence over the others. There must first be expiation made ere man can enjoy acceptance with God, or worship him. The question of sin must first be settled before there can be communion or service. How are we to account for the arrangement in Leviticus?

(1) The sin-sacrifices, though last in the order of institution, were first in the order of presentation; for example, Exodus 29; Leviticus 8, 9; II. Chronicles 29, etc. In all these passages the sin-offerings invariably precede the sweet-savor sacrifices.

(2) There appears to be a typical significance in the order in which the offerings are described in these chapters of Leviticus: namely, voluntary devotion (Lev. 1:3) is prerequisite to expiation. The institution of these sacrifices gives us certain aspects of the work of Christ. In the order in which they are instituted in Leviticus 1–7, the sweet-savor offerings are mentioned first because Christ, the great Antitype of all the sacrifices, first gave himself in perfect obedience to God before he became sin for us on the cross. He was first of all, in his life of complete and perfect obedience to God, everything typified by the burnt-, meat-, and peace-offerings;

and the very fact of his being thus perfect fitted him to be the Sin-sacrifice. This appears to be the truth symbolized by the arrangement of the offerings in these chapters. And a very precious truth it is. In his life Jesus fulfilled the precepts of the divine law; in his death he bore its awful penalty. Both were necessary in order to our salvation. His life, I cannot but believe, is the blessed realization of what was dimly shadowed forth by the "sweet-savour offerings." In all that he was and in all that he did he glorified God. What more remarkable feature, morally, can there be than this: a Person who, while he was everything, was content to be nothing; who, while he was man here below and heir of all things, never acted upon his own independent title; who always, under every circumstance, great or small, sought and was subject to his Father's will? And the Father took infinite delight in him — testified once and again that he was "well pleased with him." No doubt the Father was well pleased in his death also; but we must remember that he did not manifest his complacency in him as he hung suspended on the cross. There he hid his face from him. But in his life of perfect devotion to him the Father beheld and enjoyed "an odour of a sweet smell." Nor was the delight of the Son any less or different. In contemplating the Saviour as he is revealed to us in the sacrifices of the tabernacle, let no one think of him as a reluctant and struggling victim led to the slaughter. God forbid! His own exultant language is: "Wherefore, when he cometh into the world, he saith, Sacrifice and offering thou wouldest not, but a body hast thou prepared me: in burnt offerings and sacrifices for sin thou hast had no pleasure. Then said I, Lo, I come (in the volume of the book it is written of me,) to do thy will, O God" (Heb. 10:5-7; cf. Ps. 40:8).

8. *Ceremonial perfection was required in the sacrifices.* Repeatedly and emphatically the law declares that the offering must be "without blemish." Even in the case of the meat-offering the chief ingredient is described as "fine flour," that is, flour of the best quality. Leviticus 22:19-25 designates the animals to be employed in sacrifice, and enumerates the several defects which disqualified for such service. The prescribed victims are "beeves," "sheep," "goats" (v. 19), and in cases of extreme poverty turtle-doves and young pigeons (Lev. 5:7). The sacrifices were to be "perfect," that is, free from disease, from any natural deformity, and from mutilation. To offer an unclean or defective sacrifice would have been a violation of the law and a misrepresenta-

tion of the aim of the rite, and would have incurred the Divine displeasure. Malachi charged the Jews of his time with offering to God "polluted bread," and with reserving the faultless for themselves, thereby provoking his curse (Mal. 1 : 7, 13, 14). God claims the purest and the best from his people. Nothing suits his presence but what is perfect. The worship which is sincere and true is alone acceptable with him.

As the object of the sacrifices was to effect symbolic reconciliation with God, only a perfect victim of the prescribed class could be laid on his altar. The sacrifices were pictures of the person and work of the Lord Jesus Christ. The type must of necessity match, in certain important particulars, the Antitype. As Christ, the great Antitype, was morally perfect, so must that be ceremonially perfect which represented him. For "type and antitype do not mean different things under the same form, but the same things under different forms."[1] He "offered himself without spot to God" (Heb. 9 : 14). He was "a lamb without blemish and without spot" (I. Pet. 1 : 19). He was "holy, harmless, undefiled, separate from sinners" (Heb. 7 : 26). And the types must likewise be pure, unblemished. Fairbairn's golden rule holds here, as in so many similar cases:

[1] Cave.

"Nothing in itself evil can be a type of that which in itself is good."

The physical defects that disqualified an animal from being an offering to God correspond closely with those which excluded from the exercise of the priestly office (Lev. 21: 17-21). Priest and offering alike were to be perfect of their kind. What they were physically and ceremonially Christ is personally and intrinsically—"without spot and blameless."

I. THE "SWEET-SAVOUR" OFFERINGS.

1. *The Burnt-Offering.*
(Leviticus 1.)

The burnt-offering heads the list because it was the principal offering in the Jewish ritual, and because it had some of the distinctive features of all the others. It was the daily sacrifice which morning and evening was presented to Jehovah on the brazen altar; hence called the "continual burnt offering" (Ex. 29: 42). Besides, the burnt-offering seems to have been the prevalent sacrifice in the times preceding Moses. It was this which Abraham and Job offered; this also probably that Abel observed. It seems evident likewise that in those times it was of the nature of a sin-sacrifice; the latter did not exist as a distinct institution. Moses really introduced the sin-sacrifices; and he, in fact, gave to all the offerings the special character which they bore in the Jewish system.

(1) *Its Varieties.* The burnt-offering consisted of three grades: it might be a victim of the herd, or of the flocks, or of the fowls (Lev. 1 : 3, 10, 14). God's gracious provision to meet the circumstances and needs of his people was seen in this variety. Poverty could bar no one from offering the sacrifice and participating in the blessing. If unable to present a bullock or a lamb, a pigeon or dove was within his reach, and was just as acceptable as the more costly gift. It was the lowest grade of the burnt-offering, it would appear, that Joseph and Mary laid upon the altar at Jerusalem when they redeemed the child Jesus according to the law (Luke 2 : 22-24), an incidental proof of that great word of Paul, "For ye know the grace of our Lord Jesus Christ, that, though he was rich, yet for your sakes he became poor, that ye through his poverty might be rich" (II. Cor. 8 : 9).

(2) *Ceremony of the Offering.* The animal sacrificed must, in accordance with the high rank of the offering, be a male without blemish, taken from among the most perfect of the beasts of sacrifice. If the animal were not perfect of its kind, it would not serve the moral or the typical purpose for which it had been selected. It is

worthy of note that the same word which the Septuagint translators used for "without blemish" (ἄμωμος) is applied to Christ (Heb. 9:14; I. Pet. 1:19). The offerer then came with his offering to the door of the tabernacle, and stood face to face with the brazen altar. Here he was "before the Lord." The object of his approach was to find "acceptance with the Lord," and to worship. These words, "before the Lord," which occur three times in Lev. 1, are of profoundest import. The Lord and the offerer meet here at the altar. The question of sin is here to be settled, the claims of the Lord upon the offerer are to be recognized and met, and reconciliation effected. At this point the priest approached, and led the man with his sacrifice on to the altar. The offerer then laid his hand upon the head of the victim —pressed or leaned his hand firmly on it. The word is the same with that of Psalm 88:7, "Thy wrath *lieth hard* upon me." "We lean our soul on the same person on whom Jehovah leant his wrath."[1] This act symbolized the acknowledgment on the part of the offerer of his guilt, and the substitution of the animal for himself as the one upon which the punishment should fall. The slaughter of the victim immediately followed, and the streaming blood was caught by

[1] Bonar.

the priest, and sprinkled round about upon the altar. These two acts, the laying on of the hand and the sprinkling of the blood, were common to the burnt-, the peace-, and the sin-offerings, and were essential parts of the sacrifice. The use of the blood in these offerings is profoundly instructive, but into that subject, tempting as it is, we cannot now enter. Suffice it to say that the relation of the Hebrew people to God, both as a nation and as individual members of the nation, rested on the blood — on atonement.

Afterward, the skin was removed, which became the property of the priest (Lev. 7 : 8). The body of the victim was then cut in pieces. The sacrifice was thus reduced to a mangled mass of flesh and bones. Entire dislocation of every joint and separation of every limb and member took place. The legs and intestines were then washed with water, the various parts were carefully disposed on the wood, and the whole was reduced to ashes on the altar.

(3) *The Nature of the Burnt-Offering.* Two things, which, though really one, may yet be separated in thought, seem to be made prominent in this sacrifice.

(*a*) It was a *sweet-savor sacrifice.* It was wholly given up to Jehovah, and was for his satisfaction and delight. Three times in Leviticus 1 it is called "a burnt sacrifice, an offering made by fire, of a sweet savour unto the Lord" (vs. 9, 13, 17), that is, acceptable and grateful to him. It differs from all the others in that it was completely devoted to the Lord. The ordinary name given it designates its purpose—*olah*, "that which ascends or rises to God in the fire."[1] *Holocaust* is the patristic name. "Whole burnt offering," "whole burnt sacrifice," are other titles. The idea is that of total devotedness to Jehovah. With the exception of the skin, the burnt-offering was given entirely to God.

(*b*) It was for *atonement* or *acceptance* (Lev. 1 : 3, 4). The words, "He shall offer it of his own voluntary will" (v. 3), really mean that he shall offer it that he may be accepted before the Lord. The animal, representing the offerer, was presented by the latter that he himself might be accepted. And his acceptance was secured through the shedding of its blood, whereby atonement was made. "For the life of the flesh is in the blood: and I have given it to you upon the altar to make an atonement for your souls: for it is the blood that maketh an atonement for the soul" (Lev. 17 : 11). In the satisfaction with which the Lord regarded the bloodshedding and the consumption of the offering on the altar as "a sweet savour" unto himself, there was the pledge of the acceptance

[1] So Keil, Delitzsch, Oehler.

both of the person and of the worship of the offerer.

(4) *The typical significance of the burnt-offering* it is not difficult to discover. The words of the apostle in Ephesians 5 : 2 unmistakably point to it : "Christ also hath loved us, and hath given himself for us an offering and a sacrifice to God for a sweet-smelling savour." The words "offering and a sacrifice" may include both the bloodless and bloody sacrifices of the law; but as the apostle qualifies them by the expression "sweet-smelling savour," probably the burnt-offering and its accompanying meat-offering are particularly meant. Paul's Greek phrase here is the same as the Septuagint for Leviticus 1: 9. The verse exhibits the surrender of the Lord Jesus to God as a whole burnt-offering. It intimates that he was the fulfillment of this ancient rite of Moses in its deepest sense and significance. Christ loved us with an affection that nothing could arrest or chill. That his love might reach and save the objects of it he gave himself for us. Nothing held he back. All, absolutely *all* even *he* had to give, went on the altar of God and was for God. He had frequent and fair opportunities of gratifying self, had any selfish passion dwelt within his unsullied nature. But we are assured by the Word of truth, that "even Christ pleased

not himself" (Rom. 15 : 3); that he sought not his "own glory" (John 8 : 50); that he came not to do his "own will" (John 5 : 30). His body and his soul, with all the faculties, the activities, and latent powers of each, were devoted wholly to the glory of the Father. His thoughts and affections, his time and his strength, his ease and his comfort, his home and his kinsmen, were surrendered to God. Every journey he took, every miracle he wrought, every sermon he preached, was in perfect and loyal obedience to the Father. Whether in the house of the carpenter at Nazareth, himself often covered with the dust and shavings of his trade (Mark 6 : 3), or whether confronting the hostile Pharisees or sneering Sadducees, or weeping at the grave of his friend Lazarus, or sitting at the table with the traitor by his side, or groaning in agony in the garden, or dying on the cross, or rising in matchless victory from the grave—always and everywhere he is the obedient One, doing perfectly God's will. His self-sacrifice included the whole range of his humanity and human relations; it lasted throughout his life; its highest expression was his death on the accursed tree.

Christ sums up the whole Law in one sentence: "Thou shalt love the Lord thy God with all thy heart, and with all thy soul, and with all thy strength, and with all thy mind; and thy neighbour as thyself" (Luke 10: 27). How perfectly he obeyed, it needs not to be demonstrated; his whole life attests it. But there is something suggestive in the mention of the tripartite division of man — *heart, soul, mind.* One is reminded of the threefold division of the burnt-offering, namely, "the head," "the inwards," "the legs." As the Burnt-offering, Jesus gave to God, without reservation and without division, his thoughts, his affections, and his activities.

In the type the victim and the offerer were necessarily distinct, yet the hand of the one was pressed on the head of the other in token of the identity of the two. But Christ was both. *He* gave *himself.* He laid down his own life for us. When he obeyed, he obeyed for us; when he suffered, he suffered for us. His life of perfect obedience and of perfect conformity to the will and law of God was in behalf of his people. Theologians rightly distinguish between the precept and penalty of the law. Our obedience is due to its precept; its penalty is visited on its transgressors. And Christ has fully met and satisfied both features: he has kept the law perfectly, as the Burnt-offering; he has borne the penalty as the Sin-offering. In him *we* have obeyed, and in him suffered. "For what the law could not do, in that it was weak through the flesh, God, sending his own son in the likeness of sinful flesh, and for sin, condemned sin in the flesh: that the righteousness of the law might be fulfilled in us, who walk not after the flesh, but after the Spirit" (Rom. 8:3, 4).

In all the delight which God finds in the odor of Christ's sacrifice believers are accepted. Is God perfectly glorified in it? Then he is glorified in them that believe also, for we are "accepted in the Beloved." Does God find rest and satisfaction in the work of his Son? Then he finds rest and satisfaction with believers also, for they are in him; he and they are identified. It is not only that sin is put away, great and blessed as this truth is, but they are accepted in Christ, who offered himself to God as a sweet-smelling savor for them; and they stand in the full measure of his acceptance.

Out of this wondrous devotion of Christ to God as the Burnt-offering there springs the idea of the Christian's devotion. He is to yield himself unto God as alive from the dead, as risen with Christ. It is here, in connection with the burnt-offering, that Romans 12:1 has its profound application—"I beseech you therefore, brethren, by the mercies of God, that ye present your bodies a living sacrifice, holy, acceptable unto God, which is your reasonable service."

THE SACRIFICES AT THE BRAZEN ALTAR 147

2. *The Meat-Offering.*
(Lev. 2 ; 6 : 14-18.)

When our excellent translation of the Scriptures was made (1611), the word *meat* did not signify flesh, as it now does, but food in general. This must be remembered while we study the second offering of Leviticus, for the expression "meat offering" is somewhat ambiguous. The Revision of the Old Testament more accurately renders, "meal offering." It was a vegetable oblation.

(1) *Its Varieties.* The meat-offering had three grades: first, unbaked flour (Lev. 2 : 1); second, baked loaves or cakes (vs. 4-10); third, green ears of corn (wheat), parched or roasted (v. 14). These grades correspond with those of the burnt-offering, and no doubt were designed to meet the exigencies of the people.

(2) *Its Materials.* These were the fine flour, oil, frankincense, and salt. Frankincense was a resinous gum obtained from a tree of the turpentine-bearing species, which when burnt was very aromatic. The frankincense was not mixed with the fine flour, as was the oil, but was put on it after the oil had been poured over the flour. Salt was an essential ingredient of the meat-offering, as it was of all the sacrifices (Lev. 2 : 13 ; cf. Mark 9 : 49). It is a symbol of incorruption

(Matt. 5 : 13 ; Mark 9 : 50), as also of the perpetuity of God's covenant with his people, sometimes called "a covenant of salt," to indicate its inviolability (Num. 18 : 19 ; II. Chr. 13 : 5).

Two kinds of fermentation were forbidden — leaven and honey : "No meat offering, which ye shall bring unto the Lord, shall be made with leaven : for ye shall burn no leaven, nor any honey, in any offering of the Lord made by fire" (Lev. 2 : 11). Nothing sweet or sour was to enter into the meat-offering. Leaven was forbidden, because it contains a principle of corruption. Honey is likewise corruptible, readily ferments, and easily becomes sour. In frankincense the full fragrance is not brought out until the perfume is submitted to the action of fire. In honey it is just the reverse ; heat spoils it. The New Testament leaves no room to doubt that leaven is the common symbol for malice and wickedness (Matt. 16 : 6 ; Luke 12 : 1 ; I. Cor. 5 : 6-8 ; Gal. 5 : 9, etc.).

By the rigid exclusion of leaven and honey from the meat-offering the Hebrew worshiper was taught that only what is pure and holy is acceptable to God. Insincerity, hypocrisy, malice, and wickedness (leaven), as likewise a heart given over to worldly pleasures and to the gratification of carnal desires — the sweets of the flesh — (honey), can neither be concealed from his searching eye nor escape his just condemnation. Duplicity and selfishness in any who approach him God must judge. As there has been but One who ever offered himself without spot to God, in whose thoughts and ways no leaven nor honey was ever found,—the Lord Jesus,—he is the true Meat-offering. In him alone all that this ancient rite expressed has its ample fulfillment.

(3) *The Ceremonial of the Meat-Offering.* First, it was presented before the Lord (Lev. 2 : 1). Next, a representative handful of the flour and oil was burnt on the altar as a "memorial." The frankincense likewise was burnt. This was the Lord's portion. The remainder was eaten by the priests; the offerer partook of no part of it. When, however, the meat-offering was offered as a sacrifice for the priests themselves, no portion of it was eaten; it was wholly burnt (Lev. 6 : 23).

(4) *The Nature of the Meat-Offering.* It was a "sweet-savour" but bloodless oblation. The main distinction between the burnt- and the meat-offerings is this: life was given to God in the one, the fruits of the ground in the other. Life God reserves for himself. It belongs peculiarly to him. Hence the prohibition as to the eating of blood: "But flesh with the life thereof, which is the blood thereof, shall ye not eat" (Gen. 9 : 4; Lev. 17 :

11). The blood was God's portion, the satisfaction of his claims upon the creature; the fruits of the earth are man's, and represent his satisfaction, the meeting of his deep need.

Furthermore, the meat-offering was an adjunct of a bloody sacrifice. It appears to have always been presented with one of these, and never alone. Thus, in Leviticus 23 : 18 we read of burnt-offerings "with their meat offerings." In Ezra the offerings are summed up as "bullocks, rams, lambs, with their meat offerings and their drink offerings" (Ezra 7 : 17; cf. Num. 28 : 7-15; 29; Judg. 13 : 19, etc.). Accordingly, the meat-offering appears to have been essentially the complement of the burnt-offering. This fact furnishes us with a clue to the meaning of Abel's sacrifice and that of Cain. Abel came to God with blood. He took his place before him as a guilty sinner, but as a sinner who sought the divine acceptance on the ground of atonement. Cain, on the contrary, presented the fruits of the earth. His was essentially the meat-offering; but no burnt-sacrifice preceded it. He came on the footing of nature, as the natural man, with no recognition of sin or of satisfaction for his sin—atonement. An exile from Eden, despising the blood, and refusing to acknowledge God's claims upon him, he presumed to approach and worship God as though no propitiation were required, and he was rejected. Thus it must ever be. "Without shedding of blood is no remission." Man's best and most praiseworthy actings in nature, whether of morality, or benevolence, or philanthropy, or honesty, may receive the plaudits of men, but with God they may share the fate of Cain's fruits — *rejection*. God measures everything now — actions, motives, and men — by his Son Jesus Christ. Whatever is done in him is accepted and rewarded, no matter how small or feeble. Whatever is done apart from him, in the energy of the flesh, to please men or self or both, fails utterly with God, no matter how grand and brilliant.

(5) *The Meat-Offering as a Type.* What does it signify in the economy of redemption? That it prefigures some feature in the glorious work of our Lord Jesus no student of the Bible can doubt; for it stands in so intimate relation with the whole sacrificial system of Moses that it must in some sense be a type of Christ. Here, however, we encounter a variety of opinions, not only as to its primary teaching, but more especially as to its bearing on the work of Christ.

(*a*) Some see in it no more than the recognition on the part of the offerer of his dependence on God for his necessary food, and thankful acknowledgment of the bounties of Providence. There is some truth in this view. The word for meat-offering (*minchah*) is used in Scripture to designate *gifts* of various kinds from one to another; for example, II. Samuel 8 : 2, 6 ; I. Kings 4 : 21 ; II. Kings 17 : 4, etc. In these passages gifts were sent to David, to Solomon, and to the king of Assyria, in token of submission to and dependence upon the sovereign. But that this meaning exhausts the teaching of the meat-offering we cannot believe. The fact that only a memorial handful was burned on the altar as God's portion, while the rest of the fine flour and the oil and salt were eaten by the priests, clearly indicates that something more was meant by it than a grateful acknowledgment for daily food.

(*b*) Others find in it the consecration of the worshiper's person and property to the Lord. There is truth likewise in this view. The use of the term *minchah* (offering or tribute) in other places of the Old Testament justifies us in understanding it as expressive of *devotedness*. But here, also, as in the former interpretation, the ceremonies connected with the offering require a deeper meaning. If consecration to the Lord be its design, why was it not wholly burnt on the altar, as was done with the burnt-offering, which was certainly a sacrifice of devotion to God?

Admitting that there is a measure of truth in these and the like views, we hold that they do not express the full import of the ordinance. If Christ is the substance and reality of all the sacrifices, he must be found in the meat-offering. But how? What feature of his work does it present? Confessedly, of the five Mosaic sacrifices this is the most difficult of interpretation. Hence dogmatic assertion as to its typical teaching should not be indulged.

(c) The key to the meat-offering is found in its relation to the burnt-offering. The phrases, "the burnt offering and the meat offering thereof," "and his meat offering," etc., indicate that the two are regarded as one, the latter being the complement of the former. Bähr, Kurtz, and Bonar affirm that there is no evidence in Scripture that the meat-offering was ever presented as an independent sacrifice; it followed invariably a bloody rite. We have little difficulty in determining the main object of the burnt-offering. It sets forth Christ's perfect obedience to the Father. The meat-offering represents *the character of his obedience as exhibited on earth and in behalf of men*. In the one we see him satisfying the Divine claims upon us for our acceptance with God; in the other we see him fulfilling all righteousness, doing man's neglected duty, and meeting all his need as a hungry, starving sinner. The one offering presents the Godward, the other the manward, aspect of our Lord's work. The two are related as are the Gospels of John and Mark. In John, Jesus, the Son of God, glorifies the Father; in Mark, as Son of man and Servant of Jehovah, he serves man. In both relations he is perfect; but in doing the will of God Jesus meets man's deepest need. The Father could say, "This is my beloved Son, in whom I am well pleased" (Matt. 3:17). Man could also say, "Lord, to whom shall we go? thou hast the words of eternal life" (John 6:68). It is, in effect, the burnt- and meat-offerings.

(*d*) Christ's obedience was pure and faultless. In him there was nothing that savored of *leaven* or *honey*. Holiness and truth marked all his ways and walk. We observe in him a tenderness never seen in mere men, yet we instinctively feel that he was a stranger — a stranger so far as revolted man was filling the scene, but intimately near so far as misery and need demanded him. He did more than look on the misery that was around him: he entered into it with a sympathy that was all his own; and he did more than refuse the pollution that was around him: he kept the distance of holiness itself from every touch and stain of it. He "was in all points tempted like as we

THE SACRIFICES AT THE BRAZEN ALTAR 155

are, yet without sin" (Heb. 4: 15). In him was the fragrance of the purest *incense*. In all that he was and did God was perfectly glorified. He came not to do "his own will"; he "pleased not himself"; he "sought not his own glory." Therefore, the Father could say, "This is my beloved Son, in whom I am well pleased." In him was the incorruptness and energy of *salt*. Throughout his whole earthly career his obedience never faltered, his loyalty to the Father and his faithfulness to his people never wavered. He could say at the close of his ministry, "I have glorified thee on the earth: I have finished the work which thou gavest me to do" (John 17: 4).

(*e*) His obedience was rendered in the power of the Spirit. *Oil* was poured on the fine flour of this oblation and was mixed with it (Lev. 2: 1, 4, 5). Oil is the constant symbol in the Scripture of the Holy Spirit (II. Cor. 1: 21, 22; I. John 2: 20, etc.). How exactly the type finds its accomplishment in the Antitype the New Testament attests. The life and ministry of the Lord Jesus were in the power of the Spirit. It was by the Spirit he assumed human nature (Luke 1: 35); by the Spirit he was anointed for his official work (Luke 3: 22; 4: 1); by the Spirit he preached (Luke 4: 18); by the Spirit he cast out demons (Matt. 12: 28); by the Spirit he offered himself without spot to God (Heb. 9 : 14). "God anointed Jesus of Nazareth with the Holy Ghost and with power: who went about doing good, and healing all that were oppressed of the devil: for God was with him" (Acts 10 : 38). These words express one prime element in the type; namely, Christ's doing God's holy will among men and in the behalf of men in the power of God's Spirit.

(*f*) His obedience was rendered *for us*. The principal ingredient in the meat-offering was *flour*—bread, the staff of life. All the holy bread of the old economy typified Christ as God's gracious provision for our need. The manna, the showbread, and the bread of this *minchah* belong to the same class of types. Christ is the Bread of Life (John 6). Having been accepted through the Burnt-offering, faith feeds on him as the all-sufficient portion of the soul, and is satisfied. Bread is the great staple. We may dispense with luxuries; bread is indispensable. Christ is just as necessary for the life of the soul: "Verily, verily, I say unto you, Except ye eat the flesh of the Son of man, and drink his blood, ye have no life in you" (John 6 : 53). The best quality was used in the oblation—"fine flour." Christ is God's best gift to the world: "My Father giveth you the true bread from heaven." Christ *is* given to every one in the offer of the gospel.

(*g*) The benefits of his obedience are appropriated by faith. Let us note once more, that the meat-offering was eaten by the priests, after the "memorial of it" had been burned on the altar. Clearly, it was food for men, but for men in priestly relation with God. It is believed that the priests always prefigure believers, except the officiating one, "the priest that sprinkles the blood," —probably the high priest, who is a type of Christ. The Lord had his portion, the representative handful, and all the incense; for all the praise and glory of our salvation belong to him alone. The priests ate the remainder. Christ is the true bread from heaven, come down into this world to give life to all who receive him. We, as kings and priests unto God through him, eat of this bread, and die not. The bread of the offering was holy; no others could eat it but the priests. And who, indeed, ever feed on Christ save those who, justified by the blood and sanctified by the Spirit, live the life of faith, and feed on the food of faith?

But it is only as Christ offered himself to God that he becomes the bread of life. Without passing through death he could not be the meat-offering: "Except a corn of wheat fall into the ground and die, it abideth alone: but if it die, it bringeth forth much fruit" (John 12:24). Had he not died, he would have returned to the glory all alone; not one of our race would have seen heaven. But, thanks be to God, Jesus became the Burnt-offering first, met every claim of justice for us first, and then he became all that is involved and implied in the meat-offering. By his death he is, and evermore remains, the bread of God, whereof if a man eat he shall live forever.

3. *The Peace-Offering.*
(Lev. 3; 7: 11-21, 28-34.)

The most joyous of all the sacrifices was the peace-offering. "It was indeed a season of happy fellowship with the covenant God, in which he condescended to become Israel's guest at the sacrificial meal, even as he was always their host."[1] It was a sweet-savor offering, and belonged to the same class with the burnt- and meat-offerings.

(1) *The name* is suggestive — "peace-offerings" (*zebach shelamim*). The plural is noteworthy. Peace of the highest sort, and of various kinds, is thereby designated. It includes in it peace with God, peace in the conscience, and peace with men — the glorious issues of acceptance with God, "the rights, hopes, and duties of peace with God."[2] The word "peace" in Scripture is a comprehensive term, embracing

[1] Edersheim. [2] Murphy.

much more than in common usage attaches to it. With many, peace means only a cessation of hostilities, or tranquillity of mind. In the Bible, it denotes this, and also the state or relation of peace with God, prosperity, joy, and happiness. The Septuagint translation renders, "a sacrifice of salvation," which may mean a sacrifice either to obtain salvation, or to acknowledge salvation received. That the latter is the idea intended we cannot doubt; for this offering sets forth the peace and blessedness flowing from the salvation God has so freely provided and bestowed on all who accept it in the appointed way. The name "peace offerings" is not to be understood as meaning that the design of the sacrifice was to secure peace—to bring about peace with God. It was for those who had already been brought into a state of peace with him by the sacrifices which always preceded it. Hence it is sometimes called a thank-offering.

(2) *Its Materials.* The peace-offering might be a victim either of the herd or of the flock, without blemish, and a male or a female. For in it the effects of atonement, rather than the atoning act, are contemplated; hence there was no restriction to males. When it took the form of a thank-offering, unleavened bread mingled with oil accompanied it; and in another somewhat

different form, leavened cakes were also employed (Lev. 7: 12, 13).

These leavened cakes, it seems clear, were not anointed with oil, as was the unleavened bread; they formed no part of the sacrifice of the altar, nor was any portion of them burned as an offering to the Lord. One was "waved before the Lord," as a sign that the whole was given to him. "Thus the grateful offerer presents all he has, and spreads out his very corruptions to be dealt with as the Lord sees good."[1] As these leavened cakes followed the other sacrifices,— for example, the burnt-, meat-, and peace-offerings,— they are to be regarded as the gift of a worshiper already accepted with God and in communion with him. They were a "thank offering for praise," and they expressed the gratitude of the offerer. That they are not to be regarded as a type of Christ, appears evident from the fact that they could not come upon the altar, God's table, nor were they anointed with the holy oil. Bonar and Jukes think they figure the people of God, in whom a measure of evil is still found. The action connected with them might be taken as symbolical prayer, as if the worshiper said, "Search me, O God, and know my heart; try me, and know my thoughts; and see if there be any

[1] Bonar.

THE SACRIFICES AT THE BRAZEN ALTAR 161

wicked way in me, and lead me in the way everlasting" (Ps. 139 : 23, 24).

(3) The peace-offering appears to have followed invariably other sacrifices, particularly the burnt- and the meat-offerings. This is its place in the institution of the sacrifices in Leviticus 1-3; in the consecration of Aaron and his sons, chapter 8; in the Day of Atonement, chapter 16; and in Ezekiel 45 : 17. That is, the feast of communion follows the settlement of the question of sin. Peace rests on atonement and reconciliation : "Therefore being justified by faith, we have peace with God through our Lord Jesus Christ" (Rom. 5 : 1). There can be no fellowship with God until sin is judged and forgiven.

(4) *Its Nature.* The peace-offering was a joint feast, a sacrificial meal, in which all the parties represented in the sacrifice had their portion. This fact stamps the peace-offering with a peculiar character, and separates it from all the other Levitical sacrifices. In the physical qualities which the victim should possess; in the imposition of hands on its head; in the killing and the sprinkling of the blood, the peace-offering was identical with the other bloody sacrifices. But it differed from the others in this, that it was essentially a *communion feast.* In the burnt-offering, all was given up to God; in the

meat-offering, God had a memorial portion, and the remainder was eaten by Aaron and his sons; in the peace-offering, God, the offerer, and the priest alike shared.

(*a*) *The Lord's Portion.* All the fat which covered the inwards, the two kidneys and the fat upon them, and the caul above the liver were to be burned on the altar (Lev. 3 : 3-5). The blood, likewise, sprinkled on and round the altar, was his. Fat and blood were alike forbidden to be eaten (Lev. 7 : 23 ; 17 : 14). The blood was the life, and necessarily belonged to God; life was from him in an especial manner, and it he claimed for himself. The Lord's portion, therefore, consisted of the most precious part of the offering. It is very noteworthy that Aaron's sons were to "burn it on the altar upon the burnt sacrifice, which is upon the wood that is on the fire." After the offering for atonement and acceptance, appropriately follows that of communion. The latter is grounded upon the former. There can be no fellowship until the question of sin is settled. The first is the foundation of the second.

May we not see in this a beautiful and striking type of the glorious results of Christ's sacrifice in its Godward aspects? In his death the Father verily had his portion, with which he is infinitely well pleased. We can never fully know what that death is to him. We may only say that therein God is perfectly satisfied, and upon it he feeds with a delight which is all his own.

(*b*) *The Priests' Portion.* The breast was for Aaron and his sons; the right shoulder (probably the leg), first presented as a "heave offering to the Lord," pertained to the priest who sprinkled the blood (Lev. 7 : 31-34). The portion of the breast supposed to be what is called the brisket, was "waved" before the Lord. The action, according to the rabbins, consisted of moving it backward and forward, and from right to left; that is, toward the four quarters of the heavens. The right shoulder was "heaved," or raised up and down, in token of its dedication to God. The significance of these acts appears to be, that the parts "waved" and "heaved" were presented thus to the Lord, and then received back from him when they became the food of the priests.

The "right shoulder," a choice part, together with one of the "leavened" and one of the "unleavened" cakes, was given to the priest who sprinkled the blood (Lev. 7 : 14, 33). He was the officiating priest in the peace-offering. That he was a type of Christ in his official action seems clear when we remember that the victim, the priest, and the offering itself combined find their typical fulfillment in the Saviour.

(c) *The Offerer's Portion.* All that remained of the flesh of the victim, after the Lord and the priests had their portion, belonged to the offerer (Lev. 7 : 15 ; 22 : 29, 30). His friends and the Levites might share in the feast with him.

Obviously, this was a feast of communion, in which God, the priests, and the offerer had each his share, and all fed upon the same food of the common sacrifice. God had his share. The brazen altar was his table ; what was consumed upon it was his food—"the food of the offering made by fire unto the Lord" (Lev. 3 : 11). He partakes of the feast his love has provided for his people. And with him the priests and the people likewise feast, and rejoice together with him.

(5) *The spiritual import* of this feast of the peace-offering is quite plain, for it lies on the very surface of the rite. Atonement and acceptance, together with the abundant provision for the soul, having been furnished in the other sacrifices (namely, sin-, burnt-, and meat-offerings), God, and Christ, and believers rejoice together in fellowship. That the Lord Jesus shares in the feast is evident from the fact, already noted, that the priest who sprinkled the blood in this offering had a choice portion for himself. The officiating priest is the type of the Saviour in his atoning work. Jesus beholds with infinite satisfaction his

finished work, and rejoices in it with transcendent delight. He sees of the travail of his soul and is satisfied. The believer likewise has a joy that is all his own. Christ is his peace (Eph. 2 : 14). And he enjoys peace. Three prepositions define the Christian's peace in its Godward aspects : First, *with*—"Therefore being justified by faith, we have *peace*[1] *with God* through our Lord Jesus Christ" (Rom. 5 : 1). Peace with God denotes a state or relation. Being justified, we are introduced into this blessed and permanent relation ; we have peace with God. Second, *of*—"And the *peace of God* . . . shall keep your *hearts* and *minds* through Christ Jesus" (Phil. 4 : 7). Here God's own peace, like a military garrison, keeps guard round the mind and heart of the child of God, so that he need never be moved. "Thou wilt keep him in perfect peace, whose mind is stayed on thee ; because he trusteth in thee" (Isa. 26 : 3). Third, *from*—"and *peace, from God* our Father, and from the Lord Jesus Christ" (I. Cor. 1 : 3); God's peace flowing into his heart, and filling and refilling him continually ; peace, abiding, divine, unfailing, ever-increasing. Christ is

---

[1] On most ample internal grounds we reject the reading of the Revision, "let us have peace." Romans 5:1 does not begin either application or exhortation. The whole chapter is doctrinal. In the Greek the only difference is between a long and short *o*. That Paul wrote "we have" (ἔχομεν, short *o*) we have not a shadow of a doubt.

our Peace-offering. "And truly our fellowship is with the Father, and with his Son Jesus Christ." All communion of saints rests on communion with God. And communion with God is enjoyed through Christ, our peace.

(6) *Certain qualifications were to be found in worthy partakers of this sacrificial feast.* The law strictly forbade any unclean person to partake of it (Lev. 7 : 20, 21). Only the ceremonially clean could share its privileges. Communion is interrupted by uncleanness, by sin ; and while the interruption lasts, true worship of God cannot be enjoyed. But, mark, it was a different thing not to be an Israelite, and not to be clean. He who was not an Israelite had never any part in the peace-offerings (Lev. 22 : 10, 25); he could not come nigh the tabernacle (Num. 1 : 51 ; 3 : 10). Uncleanness did not prove one to be no Israelite ; on the contrary, this discipline was exercised on Israelites alone ; but the uncleanness incapacitated him from enjoying with those who were clean the privileges of this communion feast. He could only partake after his uncleanness had been removed by appropriate observances. True worshipers must worship the Father in spirit and in truth, for the Father seeketh such to worship him. A Christian may by disobedience or unholy walk cloud or even lose con-

scious fellowship with God, but this, serious as it is, depriving him as it does of joy in God and peace of mind, does not jeopardize his salvation. His condition, however, may necessitate Fatherly chastisements, and in sorrow and anguish he may have to learn that evil shall not dwell with God.

Moreover, the flesh of the peace-offering was to be guarded from any touch of defilement (Lev. 7 : 19). If perchance it should be rendered unclean through contact with anything defiling, it could not be eaten at all : it was to be burned with fire. With what jealousy does God protect the purity of his ordinances! It is holy offerings he delights in ; it is accepted persons who enjoy them. "Holiness becometh thine house, O Lord, for ever" (Ps. 93 : 5).

(7) *The peace-offering looked forward and backward.* It looked backward to the acceptance secured by the sacrifices which always preceded it, and forward to the communion enjoyed by those in fellowship with God. Herein it was a type of the Lord's Supper, which looks back to the death of Christ, and forward to his coming, when communion with him will be uninterrupted and eternal. Like the Hebrew worshipers of the Mosaic times, we, too, eat and drink in the Lord's presence, rejoicing in the one great, all-sufficient Sin-offering which has been made for us once for

all, rejoicing in the assurance of forgiveness through it and acceptance with the Father, rejoicing that in due time Christ will fashion our very bodies into the likeness of his body of glory.

II. THE SIN-SACRIFICES.

(Lev. 4-6: 7.)

We reach the second class of offerings, namely, sacrifices for sin. Two are described in the passages cited above—the sin-offering and the trespass-offering.

These offerings differ materially from the "sweet-savour" sacrifices which have been before us for consideration. In principle, both classes are alike; in character and detail, they are widely distinct. They are alike in this: both present the identity of the offerer and the victim. This identity is signified by the laying on of hands upon the head of the victim. This act is common to all the animal sacrifices of the Levitical ritual. But in character and aim we cannot but see a broad distinction between the two classes. In the sweet-savor offerings, the worshiper came as an offerer, —whether Christ, or one led by the Spirit of Christ,—came of his own voluntary will, and was identified as a worshiper with the acceptability and acceptance of his victim. In these, the ideas of acceptance and worship are prominent. Something is presented to God which is grateful to him, on the ground of which also he and the worshiper and the priest commune together. In them sin is not the predominant thought, as it is in the sin-sacrifices, but rather acceptance and worship.

In the latter there was the same principle of identity of the offerer with the offering; but he who came, came not as a worshiper, but as a sinner; not as clean for communion with the Lord, but as having guilt upon him which must be judicially dealt with in order to his forgiveness. In the one case, the offerer came to present his offering, which represented himself,—something acceptable to God. In the other, the offerer came as a convicted sinner, to receive in his offering, which represented himself, the judgment due to his sin or his trespass. In the first, we see how Christ gave himself for us as an offering to God for a sweet-smelling savor. In the second, we see him, the Sinless, made sin for us, that we might be made the righteousness of God in him.

Furthermore, it is to be observed, that in the "sweet-savour" offerings there is no mention of sin—no confession, save as implied in the imposition of hands, and no word of forgiveness of the offerer, except by implication. But in the sin-sacrifices we find all this—confession, imputation of the sin confessed to the victim, and the assurance of pardon for the same. All this, then, marks off the first three offerings—namely, the burnt-, the meat-, and the peace-offerings—as distinct from the sin-sacrifices.

1. *Distinction Between the Sin- and Trespass-Offerings.*

It is not easy to distinguish between the sin- and trespass-offerings, for necessarily they overlap, just as the evils for the removal of which they were provided are essentially one. A difference of opinion prevails as to where the description of the sin-offering ends, and that of the trespass begins. Not a few writers hold that the former includes Leviticus 4–5 : 13 ; and that the latter begins with chapter 5 : 14, and terminates with chapter 6 : 7.[1] Murphy confines the description of the sin-sacrifice to chapter 4, the trespass, to chapters 5–6 : 7.

The same distinction obtains between the two sacrifices as between sin (ἁμαρτία) and transgression (παράπτωμα). The former is deviation in intent, act, or disposition from the path of rectitude. The latter is guilt and failure in the sense of indebtedness. "The transgression of the law

---

[1] Jukes, Fairbairn, "Bible Commentary," "Pulpit Commentary," etc.

has a twofold aspect—the right undone and the wrong done." Redress and punishment are the two legal claims against the sinner. In the law of the sin-offering, no particular acts of sin are mentioned, but the offerer stands convicted as a sinner. In the law of the trespass-offering, certain acts of sin are enumerated. We read of the "voice of swearing," "touching any thing unclean," "violently taking," etc. The one offering contemplates sin rather as a principle—the other, sin as an act; and they are applied according as the sin or the trespass comes into the foreground. The penalty is prominent in the sin-offering; the compensation, in the trespass-offering. Expiation is the main thought in the first; satisfaction, in the second. Combined, the two offerings present a complete atonement—expiation by an adequate penalty, and satisfaction by a perfect reparation of the wrong done. Both are fulfilled in the Lord Jesus Christ, who bore the penalty due to sin and redressed every claim of God upon the sinner.

2. *The Sin-Sacrifice.*

(Lev. 4–5: 13.)

(1) *Its Significance.* The sin-sacrifice had to do so entirely and singularly with sin that in Hebrew the same term is common both to sin and the sin-offering. This clearly indicates its nature. In it

the offering was regarded as so completely identified with the sin of the offerer, was so charged with his sin, as that it became sin, was reckoned sin. This fact furnishes, no doubt, the ground for the amazing statement of II. Corinthians 5: 21: "He hath made him to be sin for us, who knew no sin; that we might be made the righteousness of God in him."

(2) *Its Varieties.* The law of Moses describes three kinds of sin-sacrifices. These are the sin-offering of Leviticus 4, the red-heifer of Numbers 19, and those of the Great Day of Atonement (Lev. 16). While these offerings differ from each other in several particulars sufficiently to justify the above classification, nevertheless in principle and purpose they are one. We cannot form a full and correct idea of the nature and object of the sin-sacrifice without a survey of all the law describes. Our attention will be directed to those of Leviticus.

First, the sin-offering of Leviticus 4; 6: 25-30. It was provided for four classes of persons; namely, the anointed priest (4: 3), the whole congregation (4: 13), a ruler (4: 22), and for an individual member of the congregation (4: 27). In each of these four cases the "sin" is one done "through ignorance against any of the commandments of the Lord." This phrase is a very comprehensive

THE SACRIFICES AT THE BRAZEN ALTAR 173

one, and may denote any part of the whole of God's revealed will. It is to be noted, also, that the chapter throughout uses this same phrase, and the fact implies that in every instance it is sin against God, the covenant God, that is referred to —not to wrong done against a fellow-creature. Here, too, we find the reason why sin-sacrifices were instituted after the giving of the law, and not before it. "By the law is the knowledge of sin" (Rom. 3 : 20). "The law entered, that the offence might abound. But where sin abounded, grace did much more abound" (Rom. 5 : 20). Sin, of course, there was before the law, and there were also the burnt-offerings and meat-offerings provided for God's people who were sinners. But when the law came, it convicted man of sin— revealed his sin in its enormity and turpitude as it had never been revealed before, and so the law made the sin-sacrifice a necessity.

The sins for which this sacrifice was instituted are called "sins of ignorance"—"sin unwittingly" or "in error," the Revision has it. This has been thought to imply transgressions not strictly moral, but rather accidental and ceremonial. But such is not the case. The law does contemplate wrong done in ignorance, unwittingly, but it regards the ignorance itself as culpable. Some of the most appalling crimes are said to be committed in ignorance, as our Lord's crucifixion; but the Jews were not held innocent on that account. The expression, as Archbishop Magee justly infers, "besides sins of ignorance, includes likewise all such as were the consequence of human frailty and inconsideration, whether committed knowingly and willfully or otherwise." These sins of ignorance stand opposed to those committed "with a high hand," that is, deliberately and presumptuously, for which no atonement seems to be provided or admitted. Against such sins the law held out a "certain fearful looking for of judgment and fiery indignation" (Num. 15 : 30, 31 ; Heb. 10 : 26, 27). These are awful and ominous words, to which every professing child of God should take good heed. To these sins of ignorance David referred when he prayed: "Who can understand his errors? cleanse thou me from secret faults. Keep back thy servant also from presumptuous sins; let them not have dominion over me" (Ps. 19 : 12, 13).

The ceremonial of the sin-offering deserves a passing notice. In each of the four cases of Leviticus 4, the victim was to be without blemish. Those for the high priest and for the whole congregation were to be young bullocks; that for a ruler, a male kid; and that for one of the people, a female kid. The slaughter of the animals was to take place at the brazen altar, and was to be identical with the law regulating the burnt-offering.

The blood of the sacrifices for the high priest and for the whole congregation was to be sprinkled seven times before the veil of the sanctuary and smeared on the horns of the altar of incense, and the remainder of the blood was to be poured out at the base of the altar of burnt-offering. The fatty portions of the bullock were then burnt on the altar, precisely as in the case of the peace-offering; and the body of the victim, "even the whole bullock," was then carried forth without the camp and burned.

The sin-offering for a ruler or for one of the common people was of a lower grade than those for "the anointed priest" and for the whole congregation. In this case no part of the blood was carried into the holy place. It was sprinkled on the horns of the brazen altar and poured out at its base. Nor was the body of the victim burned; the flesh was eaten in the holy place by the priests (Lev. 6 : 26-29). But no part of a sacrifice of which the blood had been sprinkled within the sanctuary could be eaten (v. 30).

Just what is meant by the eating of the sin-offering of the lower grade is not easily determined. Some think it was a kind of eating of the sin, so bearing it and making it their own. It is called "most holy," but this it could not be if it were still charged with sin, for then it must have been regarded as most polluted. The body of the sin-offering of the higher grade could not come on God's table, the altar; for it was accounted sin, and hence was burned without the camp. Every spot of blood from a sin-offering even of the lower grade on a garment or vessel conveyed defilement as being loaded with sin, and all such garments and vessels had to be washed and scoured or broken (Lev. 6 : 27, 28). The eating, therefore, could not symbolize the expiation proper; *that* was set forth by the death of the victim, the sprinkling of its blood, and the consumption of the carcass by fire. It exhibits rather the great truth of the acceptance of the offering, the pardon of sin, and the complete restoration of the offender to the favor of God. It is the *effect* of expiation, not the expiation itself, which is made the prominent idea in the ceremony. It is a sort of pictorial representation of the blessed Lord and his people feeding together on the glorious results of his redeeming work.[1]

[1] This view of the eating of the sin-offering by the priests is sustained by Philo (as quoted by Edersheim), who held that one of the main objects of the meal was to carry to the offerer assurance of his acceptance, "since God would never have allowed his servants to partake of it, had there not been a complete removal and forgetting of the sin." Nor is Leviticus 10 : 17 really opposed

If we assign Leviticus 4–5 : 13 to the sin-offering, and 5 : 14–6 : 7 to the trespass-offering (as do Fairbairn, Cave, and others), then one other sin-offering must be mentioned, namely, that described in Leviticus 5 : 11-13. It is the lowest grade of all, and consisted of the same materials as the meat-offering, except that neither oil nor frankincense formed any part of it. It was provided for cases of extreme poverty, and was offered as an atonement for the offerer. For both the person and substance of the offerer are presented as altogether defiled—a mass of sin.[1] A sinner himself, everything he touched, even his very food, became unholy and required atonement.

3. *The Trespass-Offering.*

The trespass-offering was essentially a sin-sacrifice, and after what has been said respecting that, little is required touching this. The cases for which this sacrifice was presented were, first, unintentional trespass in the holy things of God ; second, unintentional trespass against man. It was for infractions of both tables of the Law, and was individual. The sin was known only to the

to this view. For the expression, "to bear the iniquity," is applied either to one who suffers the penalty of sin (Ex. 28 : 43 ; Lev. 5 : 1, 17, etc.), or to one who takes away the sin of others (Gen. 50 : 17 ; Lev. 16 : 22 ; Num. 30 : 15, etc.). The margin of the Revised Version at Leviticus 10 : 17 gives, "to take away iniquity."

[1] Bonar.

man himself, and hence was less hurtful in its effects.

The characteristics of the trespass-offering are twofold: First, the victim was a ram. "It was thus fitted to remind Israel of Abraham's offering, when a *ram* was substituted."[1] The blood was sprinkled upon the altar of sacrifice round about, and after certain specified portions had been burnt on the altar, the priests were to eat the remainder in the holy place, precisely as in the case of the sin-offering of the lower grade. In fact, these two sacrifices seem to be almost identical. Second, the value of the trespass, according to the priest's estimate, was to be paid in shekels of the sanctuary to the injured party; and in addition to this, a fifth part more was assessed upon the trespasser and added to the principal (Lev. 5: 15, 16). The payment of money marks off the trespass-offering as a distinct sacrifice. In the provisions of the sin-offering we hear nothing of money, nor of a fifth part added. In the sin-offering a perfect victim bore the penalty, a sinless creature was judged for sin, because representatively guilty. In the trespass-offering there is set forth the truth as to expiation: life was taken—blood shed; but in addition there is thought of *redress*, or *reparation*. The injured

[1] Bonar.

party was compensated in money by the offender. Hence, satisfaction is the prominent idea in this offering. In the sin-sacrifice, punishment of sin in the person of the substitute is made prominent; in the trespass-offering, satisfaction. Trespass cries for redress, and accordingly this offering points primarily to the reparation which is included in propitiation.

The work of Christ includes more than expiation, that is, the punishment inflicted on him as the Sin-bearer for God's people; it embraces also the redress of God's claims on the guilty and the restitution of all that has been lost by sin. In the two offerings we have the fulfillment of the demands of law both in penalty and precept foreshadowed; namely, propitiation, forgiveness, and ransom. In Christ sin is judged and obliterated for every believer, and he is redeemed. In him both God and man have received back more than they lost.

In the sin- and trespass-sacrifices we have

(a) God's wrath against sin.

(b) The execution of the penalty due to sin, namely, *death*.

(c) Reparation of the wrongs done against the righteous government of God.

(d) The exhibition of his infinite love in providing a remedy for sin.

4. Fundamental Principles Embodied in These Sacrifices.

We may gather up some of the fundamental principles which the sin-sacrifices embody.

(1) We see in them the important principle of *substitution*. A clean and ceremonially perfect animal is substituted for the guilty human being, and is slain in his stead.

(2) We see in them clearly the doctrine of *imputation*. The offerer "leaned" his hand upon the victim's head, and probably confessed his sin over it,[1] signifying by this act that his sin was transferred from himself to the victim, thus constituting it the bearer of his sin. This putting, or forcibly leaning, the hand on the head (an essential part of the oblation) was a symbolical act, implying, This animal is now for present purposes myself, and its life is my life. It was this act of identification with the offerer which made it to "be accepted for him to make atonement for him."

(3) We see in them the principle of *vicarious atonement*. A sinless creature is reckoned sinful and judged for sin. It dies because standing in the place of the sinner, bears his sin, and is punished as he deserves to be. And what a punishment it suffers! Its body, accounted sin, made sin by the tremendous act of substitution and

[1] Oehler.

imputation, is cast forth without the camp and burned to ashes as if a thing accursed of God and abhorred of men!

(4) We see in them the doctrine of *propitiation*. The blood is sprinkled seven times before the veil of the sanctuary—the nearest approach into the Divine Presence which the priest could make save on the Day of Atonement. Seven is the number of completeness and perfection. The blood, which is the life, is thoroughly exhibited before the Lord; the penalty for sin is seen to be fully executed; justice, holiness, truth, are vindicated, and the wrath of God appeased. The blood is put on the horns of the altar of incense,— symbol of intercession, prayer, and communion, —and the remainder poured out at the bottom of the altar of burnt-offering. There is the cry of blood at the brazen altar, the cry of blood at the veil, the appeal of blood from the horns of the golden altar! God hears the cry, and is satisfied; for it speaks to him of wrath borne, justice done, punishment endured; and now mercy, pardon, and love may flow out to the guilty one without limit or obstruction. What a parable of God's way of clearing the guilty and of maintaining his own honor and majesty!

The application of the doctrine of the sin-sacrifice is not difficult. Little spiritual intelligence is required to see it all fulfilled in the Lord Jesus Christ. He suffered the Just for the unjust; he bare our sins in his own body on the tree; he redeemed us from the curse of the law, being made a curse for us; he was made sin for us, who knew no sin, that we might be made the righteousness of God in him. In allusion to the sin-sacrifice we are expressly told that he "suffered without the gate" (Heb. 13 : 12). And he is the propitiation for our sins. The profound sacrificial language of the Old Testament is carried bodily over into the New Testament and applied to the Lamb of God. All our iniquity is charged to him, and all the wrath due to our iniquity is discharged upon him. The heavy cloud of judgment which was all our own burst upon the head of our great Sin-bearer, and beneath it he bowed down even unto death! More: he appeared before God, not with the blood of others, but with his own blood, having obtained eternal redemption for us. In the apocalyptic vision he is seen in the radiant glory with the marks of recent slaughter upon him (Rev. 5 : 6). Two things are accomplished in the Antitype, as in the type, —expiation and intercession. In Christ sin is judged and put away, and access to God secured. By him we are brought nigh unto God, "and there I stand, poor worm," as the quaint Gambol said.

CHAPTER V

THE DAY OF ATONEMENT
(Lev. 16)

THE sacrificial system of the Jews reached its climax on the Great Day of Atonement, and the sin-offering was the most prominent feature in the ritual of that day.

I. THE DAY ITSELF.

The Day of Atonement was observed on the tenth of the seventh month, five days before the Feast of Tabernacles (Lev. 23 : 34).

1. *It was a day of national humiliation,* when all Israel should "afflict their souls"—seek for real contrition of heart. All secular employment was laid aside. The sense of sin was to be deepened to its utmost intensity in the national mind, and exhibited in appropriate forms of penitential sorrow. It was the only day upon which the high priest entered the most holy place of the tabernacle "not without blood." It was the supreme day of the whole Mosaic economy, and it signalized as no other rite in the entire complicated system did the vital New Testament truth

that "Christ was once offered to bear the sins of many," and that he has "entered . . . into heaven itself, now to appear in the presence of God for us."

2. *It was a day that imposed the most solemn anxieties and severest duties on the high priest.* "Seven days before it came, it severed him from his family and home, and confined him to the work of preparation for what was coming. He was put upon slender diet, and on the atonement day was required to fast entirely until evening."[1] "All night long [preceding the day] he was to be hearing and expounding the Holy Scriptures, or otherwise kept employed, so that he might not fall asleep."[2] During the most solemn functions he was not to wear the golden and glorious vestments of his office, but "linen garments," and he washed his whole body five times on the day, and his hands and feet ten times.[3]

3. *The special services of the day were performed by the high priest alone.* He was neither to be accompanied nor assisted by any one. The humbler duties which at other times devolved upon the ordinary priest rested on him alone. All was done by his own hands (Lev. 16 : 17). The only exception was the removal of the scapegoat, which does not appear to have been a priestly act. Even the humbler duties of trimming the lamps, reviving

[1] Seiss. [2] Edersheim. [3] Ibid.

the fires, slaughtering the animals, it is thought, were done by him.

4. *All this*, it scarcely needs be noted, *was typical of Him of whom Aaron and this day were but faint shadows.* Sent from the heavenly glory, he is seen to be a laborious, self-denying servant. No gold glittered on his brow, nor tinkled in his footsteps. No star of royalty blazed on his breast; no gems sparkled on his shoulders. When he came, he laid his glory by; he was the girded, not the arrayed One (cf. Phil. 2). Alone, too, he was in the great work of expiation. "Be not far from me, for trouble is near; for there is none to help" (Ps. 22 : 11). "Reproach hath broken my heart, and I am full of heaviness: and I looked for some to take pity, but there was none; and for comforters, but I found none" (Ps. 69 : 20). By himself he made purification of our sins; he offered himself to God. On the Day of Atonement, Aaron was alone. On the day of Calvary, all helpers were withdrawn. Lover and friend were put far from Him. All alone he wrestled in the garden; alone he hung on the cross. The Father himself forsook him.

II. THE OFFERINGS OF THE DAY.

The offerings of the day were, a bullock for a sin-offering and a ram for a burnt-offering for the high priest and his house; two kids of the goats for a sin-offering and a ram for a burnt-offering for the congregation (Lev. 16: 3, 5). Besides, there were offered on the same day "burnt offerings for a sweet savour," a young bullock, one ram, and seven lambs of the first year, and their meat-offerings and drink-offerings (Num. 29: 8-11). But that the sin-sacrifices preceded all others on this day is quite evident from Leviticus 16 : 24: "And he shall wash his flesh with water in the holy place, and put on his garments [the beautiful garments], and come forth, and offer his burnt offering, and the burnt offering of the people, and make an atonement for himself, and for the people." This passage shows clearly that the whole of the burnt-offering and the festive sin-offering were brought *after* the expiatory services. The bodies of the bullock and goat of the sin-offering were burned without the camp (Lev. 16: 27).

1. *The first expiatory service of the day was the presentation and slaying of the sin-offering for the high priest and his house.* He must offer first for his own sins before he could offer for the sins of the people (Lev. 9: 8; Heb. 7: 27). This fact indicates the inherent weakness of the Levitical priesthood itself, and points to the inefficiency of the whole system which could effect no more than

symbolical atonement. The chapter makes no mention of the imposition of hands either on the head of the priest's victim or on that of the goat "for Jehovah." But that this was done is inferred from the analogous action in all the other animal sacrifices. According to Edersheim, at the time of the second temple the high priest laid both his hands on the head of his bullock, and made the following confession : "Ah, Jehovah ! I have committed iniquity ; I have transgressed ; I have sinned — I and my house. Oh, then, Jehovah, I entreat thee, cover over [atone for, let there be atonement for] the iniquities, the transgressions, and the sins which I have committed, transgressed, and sinned before thee — I and my house, even as it is written in the law of Moses, thy servant : 'For, on that day will he cover over [atone] for you to make you clean ; from all your transgressions before Jehovah ye shall be cleansed.' "[1]

2. *Aaron next presented the sin-offering for the congregation*, which constituted the principal feature of the rites of this day. Two goats were brought before the altar, and the high priest cast lots upon them, one "for Jehovah," the other "for Azazel." The goat for Jehovah was slain, and its blood was carried into the most holy place

[1] "Temple," etc., 271.

and sprinkled seven times on and before the mercy-seat. There was the cry of blood in the very presence of God. Under his eyes was it placed, and by it the sins of the congregation were covered from his sight. It was *this* blood which made atonement not only for the people, but also for the sanctuary and for the altar of incense (Lev. 16 : 16 ; Ex. 30 : 10). But the altar of sacrifice in the court was also cleansed (Lev. 16 : 18, 19). No other spot was more intimately connected with sin than the altar. For there every sin was laid down, and there the wrath of God against sin was particularly manifested. The foulest sin and the fullest atonement were found at the cross!

3. *The sins of the congregation were symbolically transferred to the goat "for Azazel"* by the solemn imposition of Aaron's hands on its head, after which it was led away into the wilderness and let go. Most specific and definite is the language touching this remarkable scene. The high priest laid *both his hands* on the goat's head. In the other sacrifices where a single individual performed this act it was his *hand*, one hand, that made the transfer; but here both hands were employed : the hands that had been filled with incense, that carried the blood in to the Divine Presence, are now filled with the sins, iniquities,

and transgressions of the congregation, and these hands *put* them all on the head of the victim! Substitution and imputation cannot be more vividly expressed. In the marvelous description of the Man of Sorrows of Isaiah 53 this astonishing scene of the Day of Atonement finds its illustration and accomplishment. "Surely he hath borne our griefs, and carried our sorrows. . . The Lord hath laid on him the iniquity of us all." And the almost startling words of Paul come to us with an added force in the presence of this transaction: "Christ hath redeemed us from the curse of the law, being made a curse for us" (Gal. 3 : 13). A curse! Yes, not only because hanged on the tree, but under the curse of the broken law as our Sin-bearer.

It is not the intention to enter into a discussion as to the meaning of the expression "for Azazel," which is found only in this chapter. Concerning its import a great variety of opinion is entertained. It is regarded as a place, a person, a thing, and an abstraction. Not a few, principally Germans, hold that it designates Satan, or at least a demon, to which the goat was devoted. This view is thought to be supported by the correlative expression "for Jehovah," and as this undoubtedly signifies a person, so "for Azazel" must likewise mean a person. But this is a rash assertion. No less a scholar than Hofmann puts the argument aside by the pertinent remark that "it is the *lot* and not the *goat* which is described in Leviticus as being *for* Jehovah and *for* Azazel." This goat was equally presented to Jehovah with the goat that was slain (Lev. 16 : 7). To take that which has been offered to God and give it to Satan "would be a daring impiety, which is inconceivable." Perhaps no better translation can be given of the words "for Azazel" than that of the margin in the Revision, namely, "for dismissal," which is almost identical in idea with the old translation, "scapegoat." That the live goat was intended to represent the entire removal of the sins put upon its head, is the conviction of all sober-minded interpreters.

4. *The two goats formed but one offering.* In Leviticus 16 : 15 the slain goat is described as a "sin offering . . . for the people." Both animals were charged with the iniquities and transgressions of the congregation ; and the reasons for the use of two instead of one, as in the ordinary sin-sacrifice, is probably that given by Keil, namely, the impossibility of combining in one victim all that it was the Divine purpose to set forth. The cognate truths of expiation and remission are most graphically exhibited in the transaction. The slain goat symbolizes the great

truth of atonement—covering of sins by the blood; the scapegoat, their removal. God has his claim upon the sinner which must be met— the execution of the righteous penalty due his sins. The sinner has needs also, namely, the remission of his trespasses. The punishment of sin, the removal of sin,—these are the truths taught by the two goats. That the whole transaction has its accomplishment in Christ, scarcely requires to be pointed out. The very language of this chapter is carried over into later scripture and applied to him (Isa. 53 ; II. Cor. 5 : 21 ; I. Pet. 2 : 24, etc.).

III. ENTRANCE OF THE HIGH PRIEST INTO THE MOST HOLY PLACE.

Three times on the Day of Atonement the high priest passed the veil and stood before the awful Presence at the ark. No one was to be near the sanctuary when the transit was made (Lev. 16 : 17). The first was as follows: Filling a censer with burning coals from the brazen altar, and taking a handful of fine incense, he entered within the veil, and, covering the coals with the incense, he left all there, that the sacred precinct might be filled with the cloud of incense, that he might not die (Lev. 16 : 13). The second entrance was with the blood of his own sin-offering, which he sprinkled on and before the mercy-seat seven times. On the third entrance he brought within the most holy place the blood of the people's offering (the "goat of Jehovah"), and sprinkled it in the like manner as he had done with that of his bullock. He then returned and sprinkled the united blood of his own and of the people's offering seven times on the altar of sacrifice in the court, and marked its horns with the same. Thus purification by blood was made for the congregation, and for the entire sanctuary—for the holy of holies, for the holy place, and for the court and its altar (Lev. 16 : 33).[1]

Is it pressing the typology of Scripture too far when it is sought to find in our Lord's action after his resurrection, if not the fulfillment, at least something analogous to the entrances of the high priest into the inner sanctuary on the Day of Atonement? On the morning of his resurrection he first appeared to Mary Magdalene. His words to her were, "Touch me not; for I am not yet ascended to my Father: but go to my brethren, and say unto them, I ascend unto my Father, and your Father; and to my God, and your God" (John 20 : 17). This message fulfilled the strik-

[1] The sprinkling of the blood seems to have been in the following order: the mercy-seat, the veil, the horns of the altar of incense (Ex. 30 : 10), and the altar of sacrifice. Thus, the ministry, the sanctuary in all its parts, and the people shared in the gracious benefits conferred by the symbolical atonement of this day.

ing words of the great Messianic Psalm, "I will declare thy name unto my brethren" (Ps. 22 : 22). It is noteworthy that the word for "touch" (ἅπτω) throughout the four Gospels is invariably used to designate either the imparting or the receiving of some special favor or blessing. Jesus was not yet ready to impart such blessing, because the proof of his finished work had not yet been presented to the Father. Shortly after, perhaps only an hour or two, he suffered the other women to hold him by the feet (Matt. 28 : 9). It seems to us that the apparent discrepancy is entirely removed when we see that Jesus immediately ascended to the Father after his message to Mary, then returned to earth again, the first presentation of himself to the Father having taken place, even as it was foreshadowed by the entrances of the high priest into the holiest of all on the Day of Atonement. The present tense, "I ascend," or, as we might almost venture to translate, "I am ascending," justifies this view. He was in the act of doing so when he revealed himself to Mary.

IV. TRUTHS TAUGHT AND SYMBOLIZED BY THE DAY OF ATONEMENT.

It was for the rebellions against God's government, the resistance to his grace, the accumulated sins of Israel, that all was done on this eventful day. The holy house itself was brought into such a state of defilement that blood alone could cleanse it. Atonement had to be made, not only for the priests and the congregation, but for the sanctuary likewise, for the ark and the altar, that God might still dwell among the people, and his throne be established in Israel. Three supreme truths stand out prominently in the sin-sacrifices of the Day of Expiation: first, propitiation at the mercy-seat for the sins of the people; second, the purification of the sanctuary; third, the sin borne away by the scapegoat. The same three great truths are found in Colossians; namely, sin forgiven, peace made, and the reconciliation of all things by the cross of Christ.

1. *The value of the sin-sacrifice* is seen from the prominence it holds in the services of the day. No blood went into the immediate dwelling-place of God but it; none other touched the mercy-seat. It is to this blood that reference is made in Hebrews 9 : 7, 25, where we read of the "high priest" entering "into the holy place every year with blood of others." It was this blood that was sprinkled before the face of Him who dwelt between the cherubim, and whose glory appeared over the mercy-seat.

2. *Expiation of sin*, by which the demands of

the throne of God were fully met and satisfied, is another great truth taught by the proceedings of the day. The blood of the "sin offering for the people" (Jehovah's goat) was sprinkled seven times on and before the mercy-seat, whereby atonement was made. But what is meant by this term, *atonement?* It is not an exaggeration to say that without a right understanding of it no just or adequate conception of the significance of the rites of the day can be had. *Everything* turns on our apprehending its scriptural import.

(1) The word "atonement" is uniformly employed in connection with the sin-offering. Rarely is it used with the burnt-offering, and not at all with the peace-offering. The reason why it is in some instances found with the burnt-sacrifice is, that in the times anterior to Moses this offering was essentially a sin-offering, and in the Mosaic ritual it still retains some elements of the same. Atonement was the sole aim and object of the sin-sacrifice. Many times over in the law we are told that the priest offered the sin-sacrifice "to make an atonement for him," "to make an atonement for them," "to make an atonement for the altar," etc. To effect such a result this sacrifice was primarily and only presented to God.

(2) In the Hebrew language the term literally means, both in its verbal and substantive forms,

to cover and *a covering*. To atone for sin is to cover it up, or cover it over. Kahnis's definition is about as good as any we have seen: "To atone means to cover sin before God; that is, to deprive it of its power to come between us and God." The Divine Presence in some mysterious way was manifested at the ark of the covenant in the holy of holies. To speak accurately, over the mercy-seat and between the cherubim dwelt the supernatural symbol of God's presence. The ark was his throne, the mercy-seat its base, the cherubim its supports, and their overshadowing wings its canopy. Righteousness and judgment are the habitation of his throne: mercy and truth go before his face (Ps. 89:14). Within the ark was the Testimony, the holy law, the revelation of God's mind as to the righteousness that men must have in order to be at peace with him. But men have sin, not righteousness—guilt, not innocence. How can their sin be put away in harmony with the righteousness and truth of God? By atonement, Scripture makes answer; that is, by the sins being covered up from God's sight. And so the blood was sprinkled on the mercy-seat, that sin might be hid from God's eyes—might be blotted out and expunged. The blood of atonement covered the sin from his presence, so that God saw, not the sin, but its expiation.

(3) The *means* of effecting atonement was the blood of a sacrificial animal. "For the life of the flesh is in the blood : and I have given it to you upon the altar to make an atonement for your souls: for it is the blood that maketh an atonement for the soul" (Lev. 17: 11). The last clause of this verse is now universally rendered, "for it is the blood that maketh atonement through [by means of] the soul." The atonement is effected through the *life* which is in the blood. Blood is the *soul of the flesh;* that is, its seat, its vehicle. Harvey, the discoverer of the circulation, says of it, "It is the fountain of life, the first to live, the last to die, and the primary seat of the animal soul." To shed blood is to pour out life—to die. Death was the awful penalty affixed to the disobedience to God's will (Gen. 2 : 16, 17). The slaughter of the victim at the altar and the sprinkling of its blood before the face of God satisfied the claims of justice, exhausted the penalty, covered the sin, effected atonement. It was God's ordained way of making reconciliation and peace, and there is no other way. "Without shedding of blood is no remission" (Heb. 9 : 22).

(4) The atonement was *vicarious.* The sinful congregation and the two goats were identified, the latter standing in the place, suffering the punishment due to the sin, of the former. In

the death of the one the congregation sacramentally died; the dismissal of the other in the wilderness symbolized the remission and removal of the transgressions and iniquities of the people. "Life for life" was the central idea in this as in every sin-sacrifice. If the cognate doctrines of substitution and imputation can be expressed at all by act and speech, these are vividly and unmistakably set forth by the solemn transaction in connection with the two goats. By them Israel satisfied the penalty incurred by their sins, and rejoiced in the assurance of forgiveness and peace with God. The Hebrew knew of a surety by the word of the law itself that the blood shed was vicarious (Lev. 17 : 11).

(5) In atonement there is essentially the idea of *expiation, propitiation*. The blood expiates sin and propitiates God. The words for "atone" and for "atonement" are uniformly rendered by the Septuagint "to propitiate," "propitiation" (ἐξιλάσκομαι, ἐξίλασις). Ten times the verb is so translated in Leviticus 16. The very name of the mercy-seat (ἱλαστήριον) is employed by Paul to designate the sacrificial work of Christ; "whom God hath set forth to be a propitiation through faith in his blood" (Rom. 3 : 25). Christ's propitiation was by his blood. *To cover sin*, therefore, is to propitiate God with respect to it; that is, to make a

penal satisfaction for it, and so make it possible for God to put it away and cancel it.

The apostle John uses similar terms to express the idea of expiation or propitiation (I. John 2 : 2 ; 4 : 10). Even the publican of the parable had a clear conception of God's method of pardon by means of atonement, or expiation, as is evinced by his prayer, "God be *propitiated* [ἱλάσθητί] to me a sinner" (Luke 18 : 13). When, therefore, the blood of a sacrificial animal is said *to cover sin*, it must mean that it expiates it—hides it from the sight of God by satisfying him as to his just claims on the guilty. This, unquestionably, is the very essence of the sacrificial rites of the Day of Expiation.

3. *The prominence assigned the blood of expiation* is another characteristic feature of the day. From its symbolic use we at once perceive the reason for the profound emphasis attaching in Scripture to the *blood of Christ*.[1] The Gospels record his perfect life and his matchless death. The Epistles unfold the efficacy and preciousness of his blood. We are redeemed by his blood (Eph. 1 : 7); justified by his blood (Rom. 5 : 9); forgiven through his blood (Col. 1 : 14); purged as to the conscience by his blood (Heb. 9 : 14); cleansed by his blood (I. John 1 : 7); made white by his blood (Rev. 7 : 14); have peace through

his blood (Col. 1 : 20); enter the holiest by his blood (Heb. 10 : 19). God makes everything of the blood of his dear Son. The value he sets upon it is infinite and eternal; for by it he pardons, justifies, sanctifies, and saves the believing sinner. It is the blood that atones, propitiates, expiates, satisfies; for the blood is the life, the soul, and Christ gave his blood, his life, for us. This it was which he carried into the majestic Presence, and by it covered forever from the eyes of the living God the sins of all the redeemed.

Of old, in the land of Egypt, when the angel-destroyer went forth on his mission of death, God said, "When I see the blood, I will pass over you." Not morality, nor integrity, nor education, nor civilization, nor culture, nor character-building, but the BLOOD redeems.

4. *The action of the high priest on the day was typical of Christ the High Priest of our profession.*

(1) Aaron acted under divine direction. "Aaron shall," is the ever-recurring mandate. Deviation from the prescribed order would have been failure in his work and death to himself. So Christ, the great Antitype, was the Anointed — the Sent One, acted under a divine commission, and finished the work God gave him to do (John 17 : 4). Every part of the transcendent enterprise down to the last detail and infinitesimal

minutia he perfectly accomplished. The glorious proof of it is in his resurrection from the dead.

(2) Aaron divested himself of his rich attire. "The garments of glory and beauty," the ephod with its precious stones, the miter with its glittering crown of gold, were laid by, and the linen dress assumed. Christ laid aside the glory which he had with the Father before the world was, when he girded himself for the work of our salvation. He "made himself of no reputation, and took upon him the form of a servant" (Phil. 2 : 7). He veiled his glory. Gleams there were ever and anon that indicated who he was and whence—the Son of God from heaven ; but these were occasional, not habitual. He was the Servant, though the Sovereign ; the Sacrifice, though the Creator and Judge of all. He humbled himself to death, though the Prince of Life.

(3) Aaron did his priestly work alone. No other foot but his might enter within the veil; no other hand but his might sprinkle the blood on the mercy-seat. On the eventful day of expiation Christ was alone. " Ye . . . shall leave me alone," had been his prediction (John 16 : 32). How truly it was fulfilled all know. In the midst stood that cross in its lonely majesty — God on one side with averted face ; on the other, Satan, exulting in his triumph. The world took sides with

Satan. "His darling was in the power of the dog," and there was none to pity, none to help.

5. *The day was a graphic picture of Christ's work of atonement.* The parallelism is drawn out at length in Hebrews 9–10 : 18. And there are both contrast and comparison. The main points only are indicated.

(1) Aaron was compelled to present offerings for himself as well as for the people (Heb. 9 : 7); but the holy, harmless, undefiled One, separate from sinners, needed no sacrifice for himself (Heb. 7 : 26, 27).

(2) The high priest entered into the earthly sanctuary; but Christ, into heaven itself to appear in the presence of God for us (Heb. 9 : 24).

(3) The high priest went in with the blood of others—foreign (ἀλλοτρίῳ) blood; Christ, with his own (ἰδίου) blood (Heb. 9 : 25, 12).

(4) The sin-sacrifice availed only for the purifying of the flesh (Heb. 9 : 13); Christ's sacrifice, for the purifying of the conscience from dead works to serve the living God (Heb. 9 : 14).

(5) The sin-sacrifice availed for one year only; it had to be repeated year by year (Heb. 9 : 25); Christ's sacrifice availed for eternal redemption (Heb. 9 : 12).

(6) The blood of bulls and goats could not take away sins—there was a remembrance of

them made every year (Heb. 10 : 3, 4); Christ by his one offering forever hath put away sin (Heb. 9 : 26 ; 10 : 14).

(7) The priests stood daily ministering and offering oftentimes the same sacrifices (Heb. 10 : 11); but Christ, after he had offered one sacrifice forever, sat down on the right hand of God (Heb. 10 : 12). Four times in the Epistle to the Hebrews is the word "sit" applied to the Lord Jesus (1 : 3 ; 8 : 1 ; 10 : 12 ; 12 : 2); and the import manifestly is : He hath finished the work given him to do. Redemption is now complete, and accepted, and the way into the holiest of all is cleared for all who will enter. The presence of our High Priest in glory is both the proof and assurance.

SUMMARY.

Such were the sacrifices presented to God on the altar of brass at the door of the tabernacle. We may sum them up in a few sentences. They reach their perfection in Christ, for they were all types and predictions of his one glorious work of salvation. He is the Burnt-offering. He gave himself to God in a devotedness which kept nothing back. He is the Meat-offering ; for he is the supreme delight of the Father, and he satisfies the deepest wants of man's hungry soul. He is the Peace-offering ; for in him all sacred fellowship between the Father and sinful men is enjoyed. He is the Sin-offering; for he bore our sins in his own body on the tree. And he is the Trespass-offering; for he has redeemed us by his blood, and has made us kings and priests unto God, even the Father. Inquire for unparalleled self-denial and whole-hearted devotion to God — it is found in him. Inquire for blood of holy excellence and infinite value — it is his. Inquire for a table where God and the children can sit and feed together in perfect peace — it is found in him. All that the Levitical sacrifices prefigured, and all that God demands and the needy sinner requires, is found in Jesus Christ our Lord.

What did the sacrifices at the brazen altar accomplish for Old Testament worshipers? Much every way.

1. They served to maintain Israel in fellowship with God. Because of the blood shed at the altar and sprinkled on the mercy-seat, God could dwell among the sinful and erring people.

2. They served to keep vividly before the minds of the people the divinely implanted hope that Messiah would appear and turn away iniquity from Jacob. They thus supplied the foundation for the faith which, in them as in us, is "the substance of things hoped for, the evidence of things not seen."

3. They secured salvation for all who believed God's promise of the coming Deliverer. The blood of bulls and goats could not take away sin. The blood of Christ alone can. The sacrifices were a divine pledge that God would in due time provide an all-sufficient atonement; therefore, he could and did pardon and save all who trusted him. Christ is "the Mediator of the new testament, that by means of death, for the redemption of the transgressions that were under the first testament, they which are called might receive the promise of eternal inheritance" (Heb. 9 : 15). The reference is to those who lived under the Mosaic economy, and the statement is that the death of Christ had a retroactive effect as to their transgressions. "Redemption of the transgressions" is elliptical, and means redemption *from* them. Christ's death threw its blessings back upon all preceding times, as well as forward. "Not posterity merely, but ancestors, were benefited by the self-denying scenes of Calvary. The river of mercy flowed backward from the cross to the creation, as well as onwards to the end of the world."[1] "These all, having obtained a good report through faith, received not the promise ; God having provided some better thing for us, that they without [apart from] us should not be made

[1] Lindsay on Hebrews.

perfect" (Heb. 11 : 39, 40). The saints who lived before Jesus died were saved, but saved *on credit*—saved in promise and pledge of a perfect atonement being made for their sins. On the cross God dealt with their sins as he dealt with ours. On Christ's holy person all the sins of all the saved throughout all time were concentrated, and expiated, and blotted out forever.

4. They taught the supreme doctrine of **atonement by the shedding of blood**, even the blood of God's dear Son.

CHAPTER VI

THE SACRED FEASTS

NUMBER AND NAMES OF THE FEASTS

THREE chapters of the Pentateuch, namely, Leviticus 23 and Numbers 28, 29, record the institution of the Hebrew festivals and the laws which regulated them. These chapters contain the largest information on the subject which the books of Moses afford. Leviticus 25 deals with the sacred seasons and with the laws pertaining thereto—the sabbatic year and the jubilee, or fiftieth year. Israel's feasts and holy seasons were essential parts of the Mosaic institutions, and accordingly brief notes respecting them are subjoined.

A difference of opinion exists as to the number of the feasts. Some maintain that Leviticus 23 records but five—the Passover, Pentecost, Trumpets, Day of Atonement, and Tabernacles. Others recognize seven ; namely, the Sabbath and the First-fruits in addition to those just mentioned. We adopt the last enumeration.

The five principal feasts are called in **Numbers**

29 : 39 "set feasts" (see, also, Lev. 23 : 4, R. V.). Three of them (often called the great festivals)— the Passover, Pentecost, and Tabernacles—were distinguished by the attendance of the male Israelites at the national sanctuary : "Three times in the year all thy males shall appear before the Lord God" (Ex. 23 : 17 ; Deut. 16 : 16). In connection with each feast there was to be observed a "holy convocation," or solemn assembly, in which no servile work was to be done. These days of holy convocation did not require the general attendance of the people at the tabernacle or temple, as may be inferred from the fact that such assemblies were limited to *three* occasions in the year. They were rather days of sabbatical rest and worship, and, no doubt, were observed in every village and town of the Holy Land. There were seven convocations—the first and last days of Unleavened Bread, the first and last of Tabernacles, and one day each for Pentecost, Atonement, and Trumpets.

I. THE SABBATH.
(Lev. 23 : 1-3.)

The Sabbath is placed at the head of the appointed seasons in Leviticus 23 : 1-3 ; Exodus 34 : 21-23 ; Numbers 28 : 9, 10. It was not altogether a Mosaic institution. Its original enactment took place at the close of creation week (Gen. 2 : 1-3). Its reappointment through Moses and its inclusion in the Decalogue show how important it was in Jehovah's mind, and how needful for the well-being of men. The expression "sabbath of rest" (Lev. 23 : 3) is somewhat peculiar—literally, "a rest-day of rest," that is, a complete day of rest to the Lord. The Sabbath is Adamic, and belongs to mankind. It points very emphatically to God's rest, and to the rest which remains for his people, the great sabbath-keeping of the saints (Heb. 4 : 9). It is a Jewish saying that "whoever does any work on the Sabbath denies the work of creation." And it may be added, whoever desecrates the Lord's day denies or ignores the blessed results of Christ's redemption. Christianity knows no "set feasts," no sacred seasons, no holy convocations, save that hallowed day which commemorates the resurrection of the Lord Jesus from the dead. Christmas, Easter, Good Friday, and the rest are of men's invention—the product of the Judaizing spirit which betrayed itself even in apostolic times, and which now pervades all Christendom. The New Testament recognizes but one day—the Lord's day. All the more precious should this day be to all believers since it stands as the solitary sacred day in the calendar of our dispensation.

Seven is one of the most conspicuous of all Bible numbers. It denotes completion, or perfection. It likewise marks the measurement of time. Seven determined the order of the sacred seasons, and it controlled to a considerable degree the order of the feasts. The seventh day was the completion of the week, its crown. The seventh or sabbatical year was the rest-year for the land, as the seventh day was the rest-day for the people. The jubilee was the completion of a week of sabbatical years—seven times seven years, and it marked the period of restitution and restoration, when every bondman recovered his freedom and every alienated inheritance reverted to the original owner. Pentecost was the completion of a week of Sabbaths—seven times seven days. The Passover was always celebrated on the fourteenth day of Nisan. In fact, all the feasts of Israel were embraced within a week of months, that is, seven months. The seventh month was distinguished for its three great feasts of Trumpets, Atonement, and Tabernacles. The other five months of the year had no annual festival. Nor is this all. The number seven enters largely into the chronology of the Bible. Matthew distributes the whole period from Abraham to Jesus into three great sections of fourteen generations each (Matt. 1 : 1-17). The revealing angel announced to the prophet Daniel that God's purposes with respect to Israel are bounded by seventy heptads—seventy weeks of years (Dan. 9 : 24-27). Those mystic weeks are founded on the Hebrew sabbatic year, and not on the common week of seven days. It is seventy weeks of years that mark Israel's history, at the end of which time God's mysterious ways with that strange people will be made gloriously clear. So, too, the Book of Revelation is built on the principle of the septenary. Every reader of it must be struck with the frequent occurrence of the number seven. The numbers of the Bible have never received the attention which they deserve. Sacred arithmetic, so full of profound instruction, still waits some competent and prudent expounder.

For all this varied use of *seven* the Sabbath is the basis and the key. God has made it the center of his wondrous chronology. All the great biblical cycles are multiples of seven; for example, 70 (the period of Judah's captivity), 490, 1260, 2520, etc. It may be that the number seven is more deeply imbedded in the time-history of our planet, and even of the universe, than we imagine.

II. THE PASSOVER.

The first great feast was the Passover, which combined in it the idea both of sacrifice (in reality, the sin-offering) and festival, for with it was joined the Feast of Unleavened Bread. It was instituted in Egypt on the 14th of Nisan, the first month of the sacred year (Ex. 12 : 2), and it was at once the sign and seal of Israel's protection from judgment and redemption from bondage. The main feature of it was the lamb slain and the sprinkling of the blood on the lintels and door-posts of the Hebrew houses. This was God's solemn pledge of safety and immunity from the messenger of death, the angel-destroyer. Jehovah's word to the people about the blood was, "When I see the blood, I will pass over you, and there shall no plague be upon you to destroy you, when I smite the land of Egypt" (Ex. 12 : 13, R. V.). Redemption by blood is the solemn lesson and the central truth in the Passover. How a man like Oehler can deny the vicarious death of the lamb is strange indeed, for this is the essence of the whole transaction. The lamb died that the first-born of each Hebrew family might not die. The blood sheltered every house where it was found. "And the blood shall be to you for a token upon the houses where ye are," was the Lord's word to his people in Egypt. The typical character of the Passover is distinctly recognized in the New Testament: "For even Christ our passover is sacrificed for us" (I. Cor.

5 : 7). The *lamb slain* was the first great object held up to Israel about to be redeemed. "Behold the Lamb of God," is the cry that first reaches a sinner's ear and a sinner's heart. Christ and him crucified is the one supreme object in God's plan of redemption.

The Feast of Unleavened Bread was a continuation of the Passover, and followed it on the next day, and continued for a week. From the beginning of Passover all leaven was rigorously banished from the houses of the Hebrews. So strict was the law that the Jews made search for leaven with lighted lamp, that no particle of it might remain concealed. The name "Passover" in the New Testament is applied to the whole paschal feast. This fact must be borne in mind particularly in the study of the last Passover observed by our Lord and his disciples. In John 18 : 28 we are told that the Jews refused to enter Pilate's judgment hall lest they should contract defilement and thus be unfitted to eat the passover. It was the *chagigah*, or second meal (the paschal lamb being the first), which was eaten on the first day of Unleavened Bread, 15th of Nisan, to which reference is made.[1]

The Passover subsequent to the exodus was strictly a memorial festival. Its design was to

[1] Edersheim.

keep vividly in the national mind the remembrance of the glorious deliverance from bondage. In this respect, as well as in many others, the Lord's Supper bears a close resemblance to the ancient Hebrew feast. It was on the night of the Passover that the supper was instituted; and it was instituted at the drinking of the *third cup* of the Passover. Four cups were drunk in connection with the paschal feast. The first was drunk after the prayer of thanksgiving; the second, after the first part of the "Great Hallel" (Ps. 113, 114) was sung; the third, just after the eating of the paschal lamb; and the fourth, in connection with the second part of "Hallel" (Ps. 115–118). It is suggestive that the third cup of the Passover bore the name, "the cup of blessing,"—the name which Paul applies to the Christian cup (I. Cor. 10 : 16). Both these ordinances are retrospective: the first looked back to the mighty deliverance from Egypt; the second looks backward to the advent of the Messiah in humiliation, when he died the Just for the unjust, that he might bring us to God. Both are prospective: the Passover looked forward to the coming of Messiah as the Lamb of God; the supper looks forward to his appearing in glory. Its language is, "till he come." The Passover commemorated redemption from a pitiless tyranny—from the weary brick-kilns, and the hiss of the taskmaster's cruel lash. It meant, too, introduction into the Land of Promise, the peaceful enjoyment of home and rest. He brought them out that he might bring them in (Deut. 6 : 23). The Lord's Supper commemorates redemption from the greater despotism of sin, and from all sin's frightful consequences, and introduction into and establishment in the inheritance which is unfailing and inalienable.

III. THE FEAST OF FIRST-FRUITS.
(Lev. 23 : 9-14.)

This feast was observed during the week of Unleavened Bread. Yet that it was a distinct and characteristic ordinance appears evident from the language with which it is introduced : "And the Lord spake unto Moses, saying, Speak unto the children of Israel, and say unto them" (Lev. 23 : 9, 10),—a formula that invariably opens a new section, and marks an additional appointment. The revisers of the Old Testament begin a paragraph of the chapter with these words.

The rite contemplates settlement in the land ; it is not a wilderness provision. On the same day the passover was killed (Nisan 14), "delegates marked out the spot in the grain field whence the sheaf of first-fruits was to be reaped." On the following day (Nisan 15), at sunset, three men were sent to the selected field, and, in the presence of witnesses, cut the ears of grain (barley) before marked, and brought them into the sanctuary. On the next day (Nisan 16), the third day, the sheaf was waved before the Lord, "to be accepted for you"; that is, it was vicarious, the devotion of the whole crop to Jehovah, and the earnest and guaranty of the entire harvest. The expression, "the morrow after the sabbath," is somewhat difficult, but if it is to be taken in the usual sense, as the seventh day, then this ancient type of the wave-sheaf was remarkably fulfilled in the resurrection of Christ from the dead. For on Thursday of Passion Week the Passover was observed; Friday the sheaf was cut from the field —the day on which Jesus was "cut off"; Saturday (Sabbath) he lay in the tomb, and on "the morrow after the sabbath" he arose from the dead.

It is from this wave-sheaf of the first-fruits that the very suggestive expression of Paul is taken, "Christ the first-fruits" (I. Cor. 15: 20, 23). The sheaf was the pledge and the sample of the ingathering of the entire harvest. On the predetermined day Christ our Passover was sacrificed for us. On the third day, "the morrow after the sabbath," the appointed "first day of the week," he rose from the dead and became the first-fruits of them that slept. In him was no leaven—

no sin ; in his life and death and resurrection he was "for a sweet savour unto the Lord." His resurrection is the earnest and the pledge of ours. The great argument of I. Corinthians 15 is almost solely taken up with the security which that mighty event affords for our faith. And the triumphant conclusion of the Holy Spirit is, "But now is Christ risen from the dead, and become the first-fruits of them that slept."

It is instructive to note that the first religious acts of the Hebrews after the passage of the Jordan were the observance of the Passover and the waving of the sheaf of first-fruits of the barley which they found already ripe for the sickle (Josh. 5 : 10, 11). Thus they held aloft the two distinctive types of the Lord's death and resurrection, and signalized their hope in Him who was to come — the Greater than Moses, the true Joshua, who has delivered his people and who will in due time bring them all into the heavenly Canaan, in the deathless beauty of resurrection glory. Two precious types are thus found in the Passover and the feast that was connected with it — the death and resurrection of the Lord Jesus.

IV. PENTECOST.
(Lev. 23 : 15-21.)

The usual formula, "And the Lord spake unto Moses, saying" (Lev. 23 : 1, 9, 23, etc.), is here omitted, owing to the close connection of the wave-sheaf of the Passover with the two wave-loaves of this feast. Both refer to the harvest, the former to the first ripe grain of the barley field, and the latter to the first-fruits of the wheat harvest. The Jews hold that Pentecost was fifty days after the giving of the law at Sinai, and that it was instituted to commemorate that event. This belief has only traditional ground. The Bible furnishes no hint that Pentecost was designed to perpetuate the majestic scenes enacted at Sinai. It was much more nearly related to the Passover than to the promulgation of the law. It was observed on the fiftieth day after the wave-sheaf (v. 15), that is, about the end of May, or first of June. It was reckoned by Sabbaths—a week of weeks; accordingly, the fiftieth day may be called the eighth day, "the morrow after the sabbath," which would correspond with the first day of the week. It is remarkable how prominently the first day of the week, the day of resurrection, shines forth in these old ceremonies. In fulfillment of the prediction in the wave-sheaf, Christ rose from the dead on the first day of the week. On the fiftieth day, that is, the eighth day, or first day, the Holy Spirit was bestowed in fulfillment of the prediction of the wave-loaves, and the Christian church was formally organized into one body.

In the two great feasts that lasted each a week (Passover and Tabernacles), the *octave*, or eighth day (which is a kind of first day of the week), was always "a high day." These facts furnish no small proof that Christians are right in keeping this day as the Lord's day. Already in Moses' time God was planning and drafting the ritual of his people so that the change from the seventh to the first day of the week as the day of rest should be foreshadowed and pre-announced, for Christ in his death and resurrection is the supreme object of all his gracious purposes.[1]

The main feature of the Pentecost was the waving of the two loaves before the Lord. The loaves were prepared from the grain of the new crop, and were called the "first-fruits." They were made with *leaven*. In this respect they dif-

[1] What we name the first day of the week was the eighth day with the Jews. The Sabbath (Saturday) ended their week, as the Lord's day begins ours. The "eighth day," the "first day," "the morrow after the sabbath," and the "Lord's day" are the same. Scripture gives prominence to the "eighth day." On it the Lord was to appear to the priests and elders of Israel (Lev. 9:1, 6) — and this after they waited seven days (Lev. 8:35, 36). On the eighth day leprosy was cleansed (Lev. 14:10, 23); on the same day one afflicted with a running issue was to be cured (Lev. 15:14); and the rite of circumcision was performed on the same day (Lev. 12:3). (See Ex. 22:30; Num. 6:10; 29:35, etc.). Did our Lord himself appoint the first day of the week as the day of rest since his resurrection? "The Lord's day" (τῇ κυριακῇ ἡμέρᾳ, Rev. 1:10) may mean this as much and as certainly as the kindred phrase, "the Lord's Supper" (κυριακὸν δεῖπνον) means the supper which he instituted. Psalm 24 is in the Greek version called "a psalm of David of the first day of the week."

fered widely from the wave-sheaf of the Passover, when all leaven was rigorously excluded.

What were these loaves designed to symbolize? Certainly not the Lord Jesus Christ. The presence of leaven in them forbids such an application. For the same reason they cannot represent the Holy Spirit. The Word of God furnishes the explanation in its use of the term "first-fruits," which it applies frequently to the Lord's people. Thus, Jeremiah describes Israel as "holiness unto the Lord, and the first-fruits of his increase" (Jer. 2 : 3). Paul employs the like term : "And if the first-fruit is holy, so is the lump" (Rom. 11 : 16, R. V.); and James also : "Of his own will begat he us with the word of truth, that we should be a kind of first-fruits of his creatures" (Jas. 1 : 18). The term "first-fruits" in these texts is derived, not from the wave-sheaf of the Passover, but from the wave-loaves of Pentecost. Christ's resurrection is the fulfillment of the promise held out in the wave-sheaf. He is the earnest of the resurrection harvest—the first-fruits of them that sleep. He is without leaven—is sinless. God's people are the fulfillment of the promise held forth by the wave-loaves of Pentecost. God's harvest-field is the world. Israel was the first-fruits, nationally, of a larger harvest to come. The church is the first-fruits of a still more bountiful harvest to be gathered. The one hundred and twenty disciples of the memorable Pentecost, when the Holy Spirit was poured out with such marvelous results (Acts 2), became the earnest and pledge of the mighty ingathering which is to continue until the fullness of the Gentiles is come in (Rom. 11 : 25). The loaves were two, perhaps to indicate, as Lowth has suggested, "the two component parts of the Christian church, the Jews and the Gentiles, both made one in Christ." The loaves were *leavened*. The type fits the antitype with utmost exactness and precision. In all God's people a measure of evil inheres. Even in the one hundred and twenty, with all the supernatural gifts and bestowments which they enjoyed, evil was present. But their acceptance with God was perfect because the sacrifice made for them and for all believers was perfect. It must be noted that with the wave-loaves of Pentecost the sin-offering was presented (Lev. 23 : 19), for sin was recognized and must be atoned for. "If the wave-loaves needed a sin-offering to make them acceptable, so did this company in the upper room need the mediating mercy of Jesus Christ, for they were sinners."[1] The Passover shows us Christ crucified. The wave-sheaf shows us Christ raised from the dead and glorified as our forerunner.

[1] Stifler.

The wave-loaves show us Christ by his Spirit gathering into one body his people whom he foreknew, and for whom he fell into the ground and died, as the corn of wheat which was to bring forth much fruit (John 12 : 24).

V. THE FEAST OF TRUMPETS.

(Lev. 23 : 24, 25.)

The Feast of Trumpets fell on the first of the seventh month,—September–October,—and it was an occasion of blowing of trumpets and of rejoicing from morning till evening. It was also a New-Year's festival, for the seventh month was the beginning of the civil year, as Nisan—March–April—was the beginning of the sacred year. Each new moon throughout the year was observed with religious ceremonies, as Psalm 81 : 3 and Colossians 2 : 16 seem to attest. But to the new moon of the seventh month attached a special solemnity. It was kept as a sabbath; no servile work was to be performed, and a "holy convocation" was to be called, and appropriate sacrifices were to be offered. The trumpets employed in the feast were probably the silver ones described in Numbers 10 : 1-10. In the tenth verse of this passage the priests are commanded to blow with the trumpets "in your solemn days, and in the beginnings of your months," language which obviously refers to the Feast of the New Moon. Soltau holds that the trumpets were made of silver atonement-money. In the numbering of the first-born, for whom the Levites were substituted (Num. 3 : 40-51), there was an excess of two hundred and seventy-three souls. God accordingly directed that these two hundred and seventy-three first-born Israelites should be redeemed at the price of five shekels each, making in all the sum of 1,365 shekels. This money was by divine command given to Aaron and his sons. No doubt, this sum was dedicated to the service of the tabernacle, and it is not impossible that out of it the silver trumpets were made. If so, then there is much significance in the fact that they were trumpets of redemption-money, and hence were signally adapted to the proclamation of redemption.

These silver trumpets served a variety of purposes. They summoned the congregation and the rulers of Israel into the presence of Moses that they might hear from the lips of God's servant words of instruction, encouragement, or reproof (Num. 10 : 3, 4). It is quite likely, also, that they called the assembly of the chosen people to the tabernacle for worship. Our church bells serve the like purpose now. The trumpets sounded the order to march (Num. 10 : 5-7). A suggestive term is used in this connection, namely, "alarm"; the priests were to sound an "alarm" when they gave the order for marching. The term implies that the way before the people was difficult and dangerous, and hence they were to be aroused by the peal of the trumpet, and address themselves to the journey with earnestness and vigor. The same kind of energy and vigilance must characterize the march as the sounding of the war alarm by the trumpets (v. 9). Their common use, however, was to usher in the seasons of special service, the days of joy, the times of solemn affliction of soul and fasting, and the opening of each month (v. 10).

This feast is described as a "memorial of blowing of trumpets." What does it keep in memory? What does it recall? Some say the *creation*, which they suppose took place in the autumn, or at least was then completed. If so, it might be held as a memorial of the "sons of God shouting for joy" at the earth's foundation. This explanation seems incongruous; it does not harmonize with the manifest design of the other feasts, which related to the Hebrew people and to God's plan of redemption. Others say it was intended to be a memorial of God's voice, which is sometimes described as the sound of a trumpet (Ex. 19:19; Rev. 1:10). But the utterance of the Divine voice was attended by an overwhelming display of majesty and power. Even "Moses said, I exceedingly fear and quake" (Heb. 12 : 21), and John fell at the feet of the Lord as one dead (Rev. 1 : 17). The Feast of Trumpets was distinguished for its joy and gladness. It was on the first day of the seventh month, therefore on the Day of Trumpets, that Ezra read the Book of the Law publicly to the restored exiles; and when "the people wept, when they heard the words of the law," Nehemiah and Ezra and the Levites said: "This day is holy unto the Lord your God; mourn not, nor weep; . . . neither be ye sorry; for the joy of the Lord is your strength. . . . And all the people went their way to eat, and to drink, and to send portions, and to make great mirth, because they had understood the words that were declared unto them" (Neh. 8 : 9-12). To expound this feast as memorial of the Lord's voice at Sinai appears to be inappropriate. There is no evident correspondence between the one and the other.

The term *memorial* does not invariably signify to keep a thing of the past in memory. It means also to hold before the mind something of the present and even of the future. Thus, the handful of the meal-offering which was burned on the altar "for a memorial" certainly did not recall anything past. It was the gift to God of a part for the whole. In Exodus 3 : 15, "This is my memorial," signifies what God is for his people, and what he may be expected to do for them. So, also, Acts 10 : 4, "Thy prayers and thine alms are come up for a memorial before God": these were reminders, so to speak, to God of the existence and necessities of Cornelius; they were appeals to him in behalf of the doer of them. In these and the like instances the word "memorial" is equivalent to *reminding*, or *reminder*. It does not refer so much to the past as to the present or future. Taking it in this sense we understand the expression, "a memorial of the blowing of trumpets," as relating to what was to come in the sacred calendar of Israel. It ushered in the Day of Atonement, which was observed nine days after. That day was one of the supreme days of the year, perhaps the most prominent of all the days. It was the day in which the annual propitiation for the sins of the priesthood, of the sanctuary, and of the congregation was solemnly made. And the feast of the memorial of the Trumpets was intended to rouse the nation to joyful anticipation and to summon their attention. It was to awaken and quicken the national expectations, and to prepare the people for the great day so near at hand. It was an appeal to men to avail themselves of the provision made for their reconciliation with God—an appeal to be reconciled with him.

The Feast of Trumpets thus becomes a graphic image of the preaching of the gospel. In allusion to it the psalmist sings, "Blessed is the people that know the joyful sound: they shall walk, O Lord, in the light of thy countenance" (Ps. 89 : 15). The apostle thus writes of the ministry of reconciliation: "Now then we are ambassadors for Christ, as though God did beseech you by us: we pray you in Christ's stead, be ye reconciled to God. For he hath made him to be sin for us, who knew no sin; that we might be made the righteousness of God in him" (II. Cor. 5 : 20, 21). The force of this appeal rests on the supreme fact of a finished atonement. Since a divine righteousness has been wrought out by the Lord Jesus Christ, the gospel call rings as with the peal of a trumpet, Be ye reconciled to God. "He that hath ears to hear, let him hear."

There are other symbolic uses of the trumpet in the imagery of Scripture. It was the sound of the trumpet which summoned the congregation before the Lord at the door of the tabernacle. It is with the sound of "the great trumpet" that Israel is recalled from their long dispersion (Isa. 27 : 13). The "elect" will be gathered together from the four quarters of the earth by the trumpet, at the second coming of Christ (Matt. 24:31). It is with the sound of the "trump of God" that those who sleep in Christ shall be quickened into life, and raised from the dead (I. Thes. 4:16). So, too, the heavenly hosts are marshaled for the final struggle in earth's checkered history by the various trumpets of the Revelation (Rev. 8:2); and it is at the sound of the "seventh angel" that the glad shout rings over the conquered world, "The kingdoms of this world are become the kingdoms of our Lord, and of his Christ; and he shall reign for ever and ever." It is the trumpet made of redemption-money which calls to repentance and reconciliation with God. It is with the trumpet that redemption is completed in the resurrection of the saints and the proclamation of the world's final and complete subjugation to Christ.

VI. THE DAY OF ATONEMENT—THE YEAR OF JUBILEE.

(Lev. 23:26-32.)

Of the Day of Atonement, the day of humiliation and of expiation, we have spoken at some length. With this day, however, was associated another institution, peculiar to the Hebrew people, —the Year of Jubilee. It is of this unique enactment we are now to write. The jubilee began on the afternoon of the Day of Atonement (Lev. 25 : 9). It was appointed to be observed every fiftieth year. The three special sacred periods were the Sabbath, the sabbatical or seventh year, and the jubilee. The design of the sabbatical year was to afford the land a year's rest. It served to remind the Israelites that they were God's tenants-at-will, and not freeholders of the land. The true title was held by the Lord himself (Lev. 25 : 23). It was also a link between the Sabbath and the jubilee by means of the sacred number seven, the sabbatical year being the seventh and the jubilee being the seven-times-seventh. It enforced the lesson of the weekly Sabbath in a manner that could not be overlooked; it deepened the national sense as to the importance and obligation touching the day of rest. We are told in II. Chronicles 36 : 21 that one of the chief reasons for the deportation to Babylon was that the land might enjoy its sabbaths, even as it had been foretold by the Lord in Leviticus 26 : 34, 35, 43, that, upon the disobedience of the people, he would scatter them through all lands, and the land should rest during the period of their dispersion. Through this institution Israel was taught that neither their time nor the land was theirs in fee simple. They were God's tenants of his soil, and pensioners of his time.

The jubilee served other purposes and taught other lessons. It affected both land and men as no other appointment of Moses did.

1. *The term "jubilee"* is of doubtful origin and signification. Many derive it from *yovel*, trumpet-blast; Bonar thinks it was invented for the occasion. Its meaning, however, is given us in Lev. 25 : 10 and in Ezekiel 46 : 17—"year of liberty." It proclaimed freedom to the enslaved, and restitution of alienated property.

2. *The jubilee began*, as already observed, *at the close of the Day of Atonement.* It was after seven times seven annual expiations had been made that the year of release and restitution was proclaimed. Jubilee, therefore, followed the symbolically perfect and complete atonement. The Day of Atonement effected the ceremonial removal of the sins of the priesthood, of the congregation, and of the sanctuary. It seems clear, likewise, that the land itself was brought under the cleansing power of the blood sprinkled on this day. That is to say, the jubilee was the blessed result and fruit of atonement. Restoration, and redemption, liberty and joy, in the highest and best sense, flow from a divinely appointed atonement.

3. *The jubilee brought rest to the land* (Lev. 25 : 11, 12). So far as the tillage of the land

went, the jubilee year was to have the same effect as the sabbatical year. It seems likely that the sabbatical year immediately preceded the jubilee; and if so, then for three years there was neither planting nor sowing. There is strong evidence of the truth of the Mosaic record and the divinity of these laws in the stupendous claims and promises made in connection with them. No legislator would have proposed, and no people would ever have received, a law which thus required the direct intervention of Providence in order to its subsistence, without a positive conviction that the law in question came from Him who is able to perform all he promises, and without the belief that he had so pledged himself. Israel must have believed that God spoke by Moses, and Moses must have had the most unquestionable assurance that the law came directly from the Lord, else such enactments would have been impossible. The divine sanction is not wanting: "And if ye shall say, What shall we eat the seventh year? behold, we shall not sow, nor gather in our increase: then I will command my blessing upon you in the sixth year, and it shall bring forth fruit for three years" (Lev. 25: 20, 21). Apprehension and unbelief are thus anticipated by Jehovah's own mighty and unalterable promise. The blessing of the Lord, not their skill or industry or thrift, was to be the source of their safety and their plenty. Legislation based on such miraculous interposition of God every seventh and fiftieth year carries its own voucher with it.

4. *The privileges and immunities which the jubilee brought to the Hebrews were of the most exalted kind.* All property which had been sold or alienated, and which the owner had been unable to redeem, was restored to him. Farms and houses which through misfortune had been parted with, reverted to the original owners (Lev. 25 : 10, 13, 28, 41). The bondsmen became free again (Lev. 25 : 10, 41-54). The jubilee struck off the bonds from every Hebrew servant, and released every debtor. It reunited the separated members of the same family (vs. 10, 41). It was the time of the regathering for the scattered households. It was the time of the chosen nation's supremest joy and rejoicing (vs. 9-13). "Like the striking of a clock from the turret of some cathedral, announcing that the season of labor for the day is closed, so sounded the notes of the silver trumpet from the sanctuary, announcing that a year of cessation from all toil was come, and a year of redemption from all burdens."[1]

The benefits accruing to the people from this legislation were of the utmost public and private

[1] Bonar.

good. The jubilee tended to equalize the wealth of the community. It minimized poverty. It prevented the people from falling into the extremes of the very rich and the miserably poor. It tended to preserve the liberties both of the individual and of the nation. For it rendered impossible the formation of those combinations and corporations of great wealth which are everywhere a national menace. It tended to foster charity, and to suppress worldliness and self-seeking. We can conceive of no legislation which would prove so strong a barrier to greed as this—the certainty that at the end of every fifty years all landed property must revert to the original owners. It is the best and safest law of *entail* ever enacted: it is God's law of entail.

Like all the other great Mosaic institutions, the jubilee was predictive: it had respect to the future. It was planned to prefigure the glorious realities of the Messianic age. References to it are found in later scripture which make its Messianic character indisputable. "To proclaim the acceptable year of the Lord" (Isa. 61 : 2), is, no doubt, language drawn from the jubilee. "The year of my redeemed is come" (Isa. 63 : 4), manifestly is derived from the same. And the restitution of all things, spoken of by Peter (Acts 3 : 21), has for its basis the provisions of the jubilee.

In close connection with the jubilee is the doctrine of the kinsman redeemer (Lev. 25). Redeemer, redemption, and jubilee are inseparably interwoven in this chapter. His qualification and his duties are clearly defined. He is to be near of kin with the one whom he redeems (vs. 25, 48). He redeems the person (vs. 47-50). In the beautiful story of Ruth it is the kinsman Boaz, the mighty man of wealth, who redeems, and it is Ruth the Moabitess who is the person redeemed. He redeems the property that had been alienated (vs. 25, 29); and he executes judgment on enemies. This function appears in Numbers 35 : 19, 21 ; Deuteronomy 19 : 11, 12, where the expression "avenger of blood" stands for *goel*, redeemer. How like the Lord Jesus all this is! He is in truth our Kinsman Redeemer. He claims kindred with the whole family of man. It is the joy of Luke to trace his genealogy up to Adam, thus linking him with the race. Christ is bone of our bone, and flesh of our flesh. He redeems the persons of his people, "in whom we have redemption through his blood, the forgiveness of sins, according to the riches of his grace" (Eph. 1 : 7). It includes the resurrection and glorification of the bodies of the saints. He redeems the alienated inheritance. Our once splendid estates are gone ; gone the high freedom and the noble dignity; we are both throneless and crownless. But when the true jubilee trumpet shall sound, we shall return to our blessed homestead, the unfading and inalienable patrimony (I. Pet. 1 : 4). In that day, likewise, Christ, our Kinsman Redeemer, will take vengeance on our enemies, death and Satan. "There shall be no more death," and Satan shall be cast into the lake of fire (Rev. 21 : 4; 20 : 10). Then will follow the blissful reunion of the whole household of the saints, who nevermore shall go out (Rev. 3 : 12). What a home-coming that will be!

In the jubilee the land itself was to enjoy perfect rest (Lev. 25 : 11, 12). If the sabbatical year immediately preceded the jubilee, as seems likely, then for three years in succession the land rested from all tillage—a striking picture of what is in store for our earth. The planet is to have its sabbath. Nature now groans in pain together with the saints (Rom. 8 : 19-23). With "earnest expectation" (with "outstretched neck in eager longing," says the Greek), nature yearns for the promised deliverance. All her voices are now keyed in the minor. The very wind *sighs*. The voices of the animals are minor notes. The waves that break on the seashore moan. But these are only nature's birth-throes. The mighty *palingenesia*, the "regeneration," is promised and draws nigh. Then creation itself shall be delivered from the bondage of corruption (Rom. 8 : 21). When the Great Trumpet of the Jubilee shall sound, the people of God and the planet shall rejoice in the full redemption wrought for them by the Son of God.

Jubilee predicted these glories of the Messianic age:

(1) *Emancipation.* Bondage both of soul and body shall then forever cease.

(2) *Restitution.* The heritage forfeited by sin shall be recovered.

(3) *Reunion.* We shall "return every man unto his family."

(4) *Creation delivered.* Earth shall be cleared of every vestige of sin.

(5) *Rest and joy.* The toil and care of the present life and age will be left behind and swallowed up in the unbroken sabbath of Messiah.

All this, and much more, is the precious fruit of redemption. Jubilee, with its wondrous privileges and immunities and promises, began with the finished atonement.

VII. THE FEAST OF TABERNACLES.
(Lev. 23 : 33-43.)

The Feast of Tabernacles was the last of the great annual festivals. It continued for a week.

It began on the fifteenth day of the seventh month—five days after Expiation. On the first day was a "holy convocation," and this day was observed as a sabbath ; no servile work was to be done. The octave, or eighth, day was also holy —a sabbath. It corresponds to the first day of the week, a fact of no small significance. It was the great day of the feast (John 7 : 37), the day on which the water was drawn from the Pool of Siloam (a ceremony added by the later Jews). During this week the Israelites dwelt in booths. A wondrous sight must that have been—a nation dwelling in the leafy tents. Lessons of vital importance and lasting impressions were designed to be imparted by this festival.

1. *It was a Hebrew Thanksgiving.* It was observed "when ye have gathered in the fruit of the land" (Lev. 23 : 39). The vintage had then been gathered, and the harvest of the whole year was now garnered. Thus Israel was taught to celebrate the goodness with which God crowns the year. National gratitude is becoming, and is no less imperative than individual thankfulness.

2. *It was the most joyous of the festivals.* "Ye shall rejoice before the Lord your God seven days" (Lev. 23 : 40). "A man had never seen sorrow who never saw the sorrow of that day," the Day of Atonement. And he had never seen joy who saw not

the joy of Tabernacles. So the Jews used to say. On the first observance of it after the return from the Babylonian exile, we are told that among the people "there was very great gladness" (Neh. 8 : 17). It is suggestive that in the majestic scene of the innumerable company of redeemed in heaven (Rev. 7 : 9-17) they have "palms in their hands." The joy of the Feast of Tabernacles is theirs. "They shall hunger no more, neither thirst any more; neither shall the sun light on them, nor any heat. For the Lamb which is in the midst of the throne shall feed them, and shall lead them unto living fountains of waters; and God shall wipe away all tears from their eyes."

3. *It commemorated the tent life of forty years in the wilderness* (Lev. 23 : 43). It was fitted to recall with great vividness the time of the wilderness sojourn, when God, by the pillar of cloud by day and by the pillar of fire by night, led and fed and shielded his redeemed people. Accordingly, it was calculated to remind them of their pilgrim life on earth. It taught them that this world was not their home, no more than it is ours. They were strangers and pilgrims, with no abiding-place; and they were taught to look for the city which has foundations, whose builder is God. The present home is but a frail tent, that will soon

be dissolved, but God's people await their heavenly building—the glorified spiritual body, which shall never know decay nor death. The final ingathering, the harvest of the future, will be the resurrection of the body and the redemption of the earth.

It is both beautiful and appropriate that this feast, the last appointed by Moses for Israel, should close on the eighth day, the day of resurrection and of rest. Appropriately, it follows Atonement. Out of the horrors of Calvary springs the joy of salvation. "Weeping may endure for a night, but joy cometh in the morning."

4. *The sacrifices offered during the Feast of Tabernacles were remarkable both for the number and manner of presentation* (Num. 29 : 12-38). They were so arranged that one less each day should be offered. On the first day of the feast thirteen bullocks were offered; on the second, twelve, and so on, the number decreasing until the seventh day, when seven were presented. The whole number offered during the feast was seventy. Just what was intended to be taught by this arrangement it is not easy to determine. Perhaps thereby the number seven was emphasized; seven days of sacrifice and seventy victims must certainly have arrested attention. Perhaps, also, the decline and gradual suppression of the Mosaic

institutions were prefigured. The lesson taught here may have been analogous to that taught by the veil with which Moses covered his face, "that the children of Israel should not look stedfastly on the end of that which was passing away" (II. Cor. 3 : 13, R. V.). This was the last feast of the year, and therefore the appropriate one with which to signify the decay and termination of the entire system. Judaism was temporary, preparatory, intermediate. It was not an end in itself; it could not be. For the law made nothing perfect. The multiplicity and complexity of its rites only serve to exhibit its inherent weakness and unprofitableness. It could not make the comers thereunto perfect. The law was only to excite in Israel the deep desire after Him whom it foreshadowed, in whom every promise is fulfilled, and to prepare and train Israel for his advent.

CONCLUDING REMARKS.

The holy festivals served a variety of purposes and taught the people of Israel the profoundest lessons, some of wl ich have been already pointed out. They served to instruct the chosen people in their relations to Him who had redeemed them and called them to be his own, his peculiar people ; to teach them that they were dependent on him for life, with all its blessings and privileges, and that reverence and obedience are his due.

By their feasts the Hebrews were taught that all time is sacred. The year was so distributed that holiness was stamped on every part and portion of it. They had the holy day, the holy week, the holy month, and the holy year. Thereby they learned that their time was God's, not their own; that their property and themselves were likewise his. The same deep lesson is taught Christians: "Ye are not your own; for ye are bought with a price: therefore glorify God in your body, and in your spirit, which are God's" (I. Cor. 6 : 19, 20).

The system of feasts seems, in the chronological arrangement of them, to have been predictive. They prefigure in broad outlines the *course of time* as it relates to redemption. They begin with the Passover, that is, redemption by blood, and they end with the Feast of Tabernacles, the ultimate issue of redemption in the resurrection and glorification of the people of God, when the glad shout shall ring over the new earth: "The tabernacle of God is with men, and he will dwell with them, and they shall be his people, and God himself shall be with them, and be their God. And God shall wipe away all tears from their eyes; and there shall be no more death, neither sorrow, nor crying, neither shall there be any more pain: for the former things are passed away" (Rev. 21 : 3, 4).

INDEX

AARON, 92, 100, 114.
  consecration of, 114.
Altar, brazen, see Brazen altar.
  of incense, see Golden altar of incense.
Anointing, of high priest, 115.
  of Aaron's sons, 121.
Arithmetic, sacred, 211.
Ark of the covenant, 75.
  cherubim, 76.
  contents of the ark, 78.
  God's throne, 79.
  mercy-seat, 80.
Atonement, Day of, 19, 183, 228.
  the day itself, 183.
  offerings of the day, 185.
  entrance of high priest into most holy place, 191.
  truths taught and symbolized by, 193.
Atonement, meaning of the word, 195.
  vicarious, 197.
  Christ's work of, 202.
Augustine, quoted, 13.
Azazel, meaning of, 189.

BAHR, cited, 153.
Bezaleel, 16.
Blessing of the chosen people, 123.
Bloodshedding, 109, 120, 129.
Bonar, quoted, 111, 127, 140, 160, 178, 232.
  cited, 124, 153, 160, 177, 230.
Brazen altar, 41.
  form of, 42.
  horns of, 44.
  position of, 46.

Bread of presence, 63.
Breastplate, 96.
Brooke, quoted, 62.
Brown, W., cited, 35, 38.
Burnt-offering, 132, 138.
  its varieties, 139.
  ceremony of, 139.
  nature of, 141.
  its typical significance, 143.

CALENDAR, sacred, 32.
Candlestick, 56.
  description of, 56.
  typical meaning of, 57.
Catholicism, Roman, 102.
Cave, quoted, 129, 137.
  cited, 177.
Cherubim, 76.
Christ, our High Priest, 22 ff.
  the bread of life, 66, 156.
  incarnation prophesied, 88.
  the high priest a type of, 99, 104, 200.
  perfections of his priesthood, 114.
  his work of atonement, 202 ff.
  our Kinsman Redeemer, 234, 235.
Christianity and Judaism, see Introduction.
Concluding remarks, 240.
Congregation, sin-offering for, 187.
  transfer of sins of, to the scapegoat, 188.
Cook, cited, 34, 39.
Court and its contents, 40.
  brazen altar, 41.
  laver, 48.

243

DECALOGUE, 78, 79, 209.
Delitzsch, cited, 25, 142.

EDERSHEIM, quoted, 158, 184, 187.
    cited, 184, 213.
Encampment of Israel, 39.
Ephod, 95.
Erdman, quoted, 69.
Expiation, 194, 198.
    Day of, *see* Atonement, Day of.

FAIRBAIRN, quoted, 137.
    cited, 170, 177.
Feasts, the sacred, 207.
    number and names, 207.
    Sabbath, 208.
    Passover, 211.
    First-fruits, 215.
    Pentecost, 217.
    Trumpets, 222.
    Day of Atonement—year of jubilee, 228.
    Tabernacles, 236.
    concluding remarks, 240.
Fergusson, cited, 34, 36.
First-fruits, Feast of, 215.

GESENIUS, cited, 34.
Gold, the sacred metal, 58.
Golden altar of incense, 66.
    position of, 69.
    incense burned upon, 70.
    its connection with altar of sacrifice, 70.
    symbolical meaning, 71, 72, 73.
Gospel in the Old Testament, the, 13.

HARVEY, quoted, 197.
Hebrews, Epistle to, an inspired commentary on ancient Judaism, 21.
Herder, quoted, 23.
High priest in Israel, 93.
    dress of, 95.
    ephod, 95.

High priest in Israel, *continued*.
    breastplate, 96.
    miter and golden plate, 98.
    Urim and Thummim, 99.
    a type of Christ, 99, 200.
    functions of, 101.
    consecration of, 114.
    washing of, 115.
    investiture of, 115.
    anointing of, 115.
Hofmann, quoted, 190.
Holiness, God's, 128.
Holy Spirit, 50, 155, 218.

IMPUTATION, 180.
Incense, 70.
    tar of, *see* Golden altar of incense.
Inspiration, structural, 69.
Intercession, 72, 73, 111.
Introduction, 13.
Investiture of the high priest, 115.

JUBILEE, year of, 228.
    the term "jubilee," 230.
    beginning of the jubilee, 230.
    brought rest to the land, 230.
    privileges and immunities, 232.
Judaism and Christianity, *see* Introduction.
Jukes, cited, 160, 170.

KALISCH, quoted, 45, 98.
Keil, cited, 142.
Kinsman redeemer, 234.
    Christ our, 234, 235.
Kitto, cited, 38.
Kurtz, cited, 153.

LAVER, 48.
    material of, 48.
    form of, 49.
    position of, 49.
    typical significance of, 49.

INDEX 245

Leaven, 148.
Lindsay, quoted, 205.
Lord's day, *see* Sabbath.
Lord's Supper, 214, 215.
Lowth, quoted, 221.

MAGEE, ARCHBISHOP, quoted, 174.
Martin, Hugh, quoted, 92.
Meat-offering, 147.
   its varieties, 147.
   its materials, 147.
   ceremonial of, 149.
   nature of, 149.
   as a type, 151.
Melchizedek, 23, 29, 92.
Mercy-seat, 80.
Messianic age, glories of, predicted, 236.
Miter and golden plate, 98.
Moses preached the gospel, 13 ff.
Murphy, quoted, 158.
   cited, 43, 170.

NEW MOON, Feast of, 223.

OEHLER, cited, 36, 142, 180, 212.
Offerings, *see* Sacrifices offered at the brazen altar.
Oil, a symbol, 61, 155.

PASCAL, quoted, 13.
Passover, Feast of, 19, 211.
Peace-offering, 158.
   its name, 158.
   its materials, 159.
   its place, 161.
   its nature, 161.
   its spiritual import, 164.
   qualifications of partakers, 166.
   looked forward and backward, 167.
Pentecost, day of, 119, 123.
   Feast of, 217.
Philo, quoted, 176.
Plumptre, cited, 34, 35.
Priesthood, 91.
   universality, 91.

Priesthood, *continued.*
   a real office, 91.
   the two great priests of the Old Testament, 92.
   the high priest in Israel, 93.
   nature of the priestly office, 105.
   Christ's, perfections of, 114.
   consecration of Aaron and his sons, 114.
Propitiation, 181, 198.

RAWLINSON, quoted, 44, 67.
   cited, 124.
Regeneration prefigured, 50.
Representation, principle of, 106.
Retirement of the priestly family, 122.

SABBATH, 208.
Sacrifices offered at the brazen altar, 128.
   general observations, 128.
   prevalence of sin, 128.
   God's holiness, 128.
   God's remedy for man's sin — bloodshedding, 129.
   the parties to the sacrifice, 131.
   the offerings typical of the offering of Christ, 131.
   classification of offerings, 132.
   order of arrangement in Leviticus, 133.
   ceremonial perfection required, 136.
   "sweet-savour" offerings, 132, 138.
   burnt-offering, 138.
   meat-offering, 147.
   peace-offering, 158.
   sin-sacrifices, 168.
   distinction between sin- and trespass-offerings, 170.

Sacrifices, *continued.*
   the sin-sacrifice, 171.
   the trespass offering, 177.
   fundamental principles, 180.
      substitution, 180.
      imputation, 180.
      vicarious atonement, 180.
      propitiation, 181.
   summary, 203.
Sanctuary and its furniture, 55.
   candlestick, 56.
   table of showbread, 62.
   golden altar of incense, 66.
   veil, 73.
   ark of the covenant, 75.
Scapegoat, 188.
Sciss, quoted, 184.
Seven, the number, 210.
Showbread, table of, 62.
Sin, prevalence of, 128.
   God's remedy for, 129.
   expiation of, 194, 198.
Sin-sacrifice, 171.
   its significance, 171.
   its varieties, 172.
   value of, 194.
Sin-sacrifices, *see* Sacrifices offered at the brazen altar.
Soltau, cited, 35, 97, 223.
Stifler, quoted, 221.
Substitution, 180.
Sweet-savor offerings, *see* Sacrifices offered at the brazen altar.

TABERNACLE of the wilderness, 31.
   names of, 34.
   Fergusson's reconstruction, 34.
   description of, 36.
   position of, 38.
   court and contents, 40.
   sanctuary and furniture, 55.
   typical significance, 82.
Tabernacles, Feast of, 236.
Table of showbread, 62.
Testimony, the, 78, 196.
Trespass-offering, 177.
Trumpets, Feast of, 222.

UNLEAVENED BREAD, Feast of, 212, 213, 215.
Urim and Thummim, 99.

VAN OOSTERZEE, quoted, 30.
Veil, of the tabernacle, 73.
   of the temple, 74.
Vicarious atonement, 180.
Vitringa, quoted, 107.

WESTCOTT and Hort, cited, 117.
Witsius, quoted, 29.
Worship, conditions of, 31, 69.
   place of, 32.
   ministry of, 32, 91.
   means of, 32, 128.
   times of, 32, 207.

www.ingramcontent.com/pod-product-compliance
Lightning Source LLC
Chambersburg PA
CBHW032150230426
43672CB00011B/2507